On the 3rd of September 1995 a Hollywood movie had its European Gala Premiere in Stirling, Scotland. As a host of celebrities descended on the town, led by the star and director of the movie, Mel Gibson, hundreds of thousands of people lined the streets. One old lady said that she had never seen anything like it before in her life.

LIN ANDERSON was born in Greenock of Scottish and Irish parents. A novelist and screenwriter, she is a graduate of both Glasgow and Edinburgh Universities. Her first film, *Small Love,* premiered at the Edinburgh Film Festival and was broadcast on Scottish Television. It earned her a nomination for TAPS writer of the year award 2001. Her African short stories have been published in the 10th Anniversary Macallan collection, and broadcast on BBC and international radio. Her first novel *Driftnet* featuring Glasgow based Forensic Scientist Dr Rhona MacLeod was launched at the 2003 Edinburgh Book Festival and became a Scottish bestseller. Her second novel in the series, *Torch*, was published September 2004, and the third, *Deadly Code*, in August 2005. Her novels are also to be published in German, French and Swedish.

Lin Anderson saw *Braveheart* for the first time in a cinema in Edinburgh in September 1995. As the credits rolled, the audience remained in their seats in silence, as happened at *Braveheart* showings in cinemas throughout the world. One elderly matron rose to her feet. 'Yesssssss!!!!', she proclaimed, punching the air in a very unmatronly sort of a way. The entire audience joined her in giving the movie a five-minute standing ovation. Lin knew she was witnessing something unique. What she didn't know, was her experience that night would set her off on a journey of discovery from Scotland to Hollywood and back again. Along the way she would unearth a wealth of stories and history about *Braveheart* and William Wallace. Lin and her husband John established MacBraveHeart.com in 1995.

By the same author:

Driftnet (Luath Press, 2003)
Torch (Luath Press, 2004)
Deadly Code (Luath Press, 2005)
Blood Red Roses (Sandstone Press, 2005)

*To Alanna
with love*

BRAVEHEART
From Hollywood to Holyrood

LIN ANDERSON

Additional Research by
JOHN ANDERSON

Lin Anderson

Luath Press Limited

EDINBURGH

www.luath.co.uk

First Published 2005

The paper used in this book is recyclable. It is made from low chlorine pulps produced in a low energy, low emission manner from renewable forests.

Printed and bound by
Scotprint, Haddington

Cover images — Front cover, clockwise from left: Mel Gibson in *Braveheart* (© 20th Century Fox); Wallace Monument, Stirling (J Anderson); Scottish Parliament debating chamber, (© Scottish Parliamentary Corporate Body, 2005); Wallace's sword against the Braveheart tartan, both as used in film (J Anderson). Back cover: Author image (J Anderson); Mel Gibson at the European premiere of *Braveheart*, Stirling, September 1997 (© Whylers, Stirling).

Line art illustrations by Andrew Hillhouse

Typeset in 10.5 point Sabon and 9 point Univers

A stupendous historical saga, *Braveheart* won five Oscars, including Best Picture and Best Director for star Mel Gibson. He plays William Wallace, a 13th-century Scottish commoner who unites the various clans against a cruel English King, Edward The Longshanks (Patrick McGoohan). The scenes of hand-to-hand combat are brutally violent, but they never glorify the bloodshed. There is such enormous scope to this story that it works on a smaller, more personal scale as well, essaying love and loss, patriotism and passion. Extremely moving, it reveals Gibson as a multi-talented performer and remarkable director with an eye for detail and an understanding of human emotion. The film is nearly three hours long and includes several plot tangents, yet is never dull. This movie resonates long after you have seen it, both for its visual beauty and for its powerful story.

Rochelle O'Gorman
Amazon.com Essentials

'I hope they can't talk at the end of *Braveheart*. I hope they're so moved and inspired by this great story that they've found something in themselves.'

Mel Gibson, *Braveheart: a filmmaker's passion* (2000)

1

As I watched the movie I was completely immersed in the experience. I suspended all disbelief, and was 'there' in a sense that I cannot remember ever having in a movie theatre. At the end of the movie, I was unable to stand and simply sat and wept for about five minutes. Later, in the car on the way home, I continued to weep.

2

The movie gives the public someone to set on a pedestal, a legend born again on the screen, and I for one, love that fact. All I know is that when my children grow up, and the past is lost in the face of technology, I'll sit them down and show them the true meaning of history, passion and the past fights of the revolutionaries that I admire and love.

3

Braveheart was the first time I have ever seen my Dad cry over a movie.

Emails sent to the MacBraveHeart website

Acknowledgements

Randall Wallace, originator of the name 'Braveheart' for William Wallace, for writing the *Braveheart* screenplay and generously giving permission to reproduce extracts from it. Also for attendance at the *Braveheart* Convention 1997

Andrew Weir (YOUNG HAMISH)

James Robinson (YOUNG WILLIAM)

Mhairi Culvey (YOUNG MURRON)

The late Ian Bannen (THE LEPER), and his wife Marilyn

Brendan Gleeson (ADULT HAMISH)

Julia Austin (THE BRIDE)

Sandy Nelson (JOHN WALLACE)

David R. Ross and Willie Douglas of the Society of William Wallace

Elspeth King of the Stirling Smith Museum & Art Gallery

Alan Smart of the Scottish Parliament

Seoras, Pamela, and the Wallace Clan Trust

Dr Fiona Watson of Stirling University

Blaithin Fitzgerald for information on *Braveheart* filming in Ireland

Andrew Hillhouse for his *Braveheart* artwork

Linda MacDonald Lewis and family

Sue Ritchie of Phoenix Arizona

And a special thank you to all the Bravehearters round the world who continue to share their stories with us via the MacBraveHeart website.

Contents

Foreword

You've come to the right place then...

Sitting majestically on the divide between lowland and highland Scotland, Stirling was an unlikely location for a Hollywood premiere. Before *Braveheart* few remembered its unique position in the turbulent history of Scotland. Few were aware that on 11 September 1297, at this place, between the sweep of the Castle rock and the rise of the Abbey Craig on the opposite bank of the river Forth, was fought the battle that defined Scotland's future as an independent nation. In this battle of Stirling Bridge, *Braveheart*'s hero, William Wallace, was joint leader in a successful stand against the then mightiest army in Christendom. The hero and the victory are commemorated in the National Wallace Monument, which stands on the Abbey Craig overlooking the battlefield. Ten years and much debate later, the movie that premiered in Stirling stands as an even more significant monument to the enduring story of William Wallace, and to the fight for freedom both in Scotland, and wherever this fight needs to be fought.

Braveheart has captured the hearts and minds of millions of people of all nationalities in a unique and powerful way. Anything with such a degree of power and impact will inevitably attract criticism from some quarters, and *Braveheart* has been no exception. Journalists and academics from the fields of history, media studies and politics wrote disparagingly about *Braveheart* despite the overwhelmingly positive public response to the movie.

Braveheart rose above the accusation of national embarrassment to give voice to the Scotland of the new Millennium. On 1 July 1999, national television coverage of the opening of the new Scottish Parliament began and ended to the sound of James

Horner's *Braveheart* soundtrack music, testimony to the way that Hollywood's retelling of the Wallace story has entered the Scottish subconscious to stay. As the Parliament opened, Twentieth Century Fox released a special commemorative *Braveheart* video boxed set. At the official opening of the new Scottish Parliament building at Holyrood on 9 October 2004, Phil Horwood, a member of the security staff, wore the Braveheart Warrior tartan, to carry in the Mace, presented by Her Majesty the Queen.

The *Braveheart* phenomenon is ongoing. Through the Mac-BraveHeart website, started in 1995, we continue to collect the often moving testimonies of people from all over the world, many of which feature on these pages.

More than anything, this book is the people's story of the movie that took a nation by surprise and the world by storm.

Lin Anderson
August 2005

Chapter One

The *Braveheart* Phenomenon

Now, we're on the field in Ireland and we're making *Braveheart* and there's three thousand insane Irish men, which is a redundant term. And they're there and they can feel the power of the moment. Mel is riding up and down making the speech at Stirling. 'You've come to fight as free men and free men you are.' The horse could smell Mel's adrenaline and his voice is ripping from his throat. Everyone on the field could feel the power of it. The Clan Wallace was in the middle and the Irish army was stretched out on either side and Mel was screaming this speech and what was supposed to happen at that moment was, he says, 'and what will you do with that freedom, will you fight?' And that's the moment in the movie when the two who have been leading the mutiny step forward and say 'no, against those odds we'll run and we'll live.' That's what was supposed to happen. And Mel is on the horse and he's not Mel Gibson anymore he's William Wallace. And we're all watching him. We're all feeling the power of the moment. He's riding alone, the horse smelling his blood hot. The horse is dancing and the wind is blowing and Mel's voice is carried on the wind and he screams to the three thousand of us there. 'You've come to fight as free men and free men you are. What will you do with your freedom? Will you fight?' And three thousand guys go 'Yeah!'

Seven cameras running. Cut! Cut! Cut!

Randall Wallace
BRAVEHEART CONVENTION, STIRLING, SEPTEMBER 1997

The power of William Wallace, alive and kicking, on a film set, seven hundred years after the real Battle of Stirling Bridge took place.

Wallace, Scotland's national hero; ignored, subdued, suppressed, almost forgotten, until a Hollywood movie is made of his story. [1] 'Those who did remember, know, Wallace made Scotland. He is Scotland. He is the symbol of all that is best and purest and truest and most heroic in our national life.'

> *As a Scot from Cowdenbeath, I was amazed at how powerful and proud this movie made me feel.*
> John Dillon

Perhaps no other person in Scotland's history more symbolises what we want to be as a people and as a nation. Myth or reality, the values and characteristics we attribute to Wallace, we would like to achieve in ourselves. The same characteristics made Wallace appeal throughout the world. Esteemed as the first freedom fighter, he had admirers in those that followed his path, Joan of Arc in France, Garabaldi in Italy, Kossuth in Hungary and George Washington in America among them.

> *Braveheart is a piece of Scottish history; of our history, and will be forever.*
> Celtic JDC (Scotland)

What do we really know of Wallace? We know Wallace raised his head in 1296 in a Scotland that was in dire need of a hero. Scotland, after one hundred years of peace with its neighbour, was now a country in turmoil. Edward I of England, obsessed with annexing Scotland, had supported John Balliol's claim to the throne, controlling him as a puppet king. Scotland was being systematically subsumed into its larger and more powerful neighbour. Wallace rose against the oppressive forces of tax gatherers and soldiers sent in to control and subdue Scotland, winning a dramatic victory against superior English forces at Stirling Bridge. He was made one of the Guardians of Scotland. Less than a year later he was defeated at Falkirk. As those who had stood with him were either killed or captured or had capitulated, Wallace went to France to plead Scotland's case with the French King. Returning, he was captured at Robroyston near Glasgow, betrayed by Sir John Menteith, Governor of Dumbarton Castle. He was swiftly taken to London where his trial was a mockery of any form of justice. Edward I sought to annihilate Wallace by the manner of his death, allowing no burial place, but dividing his body into pieces and sending them to hang in four places in what he now believed was his kingdom. Disposing of Wallace in this way was probably Edward's biggest mistake. In killing Wallace, he made him live forever.

Since *Braveheart*, interest in Wallace has grown in Scotland and around the world and there are now many books available on Wallace, the Wars of Independence and Scottish history for those who seek to know more of the man. However this book is not about an historical Wallace. Rather it is about the impact of the Wallace story on the people who came to hear it seven centuries later through *Braveheart*.

2 'With the chroniclers of his own country, who write after the Wars of Independence, Wallace rises to the highest pinnacles of heroism and magnanimity. To the English chroniclers he is a pestilent ruffian; a disturber of the peace of the times; an outrager of all laws and social duties; finally a robber, head of one of many bands of robbers and marauders infesting Scotland.'

The rape of Berwick, where Edward ordered the entire population of the town to be killed, including women and children, was in the original screenplay and was shot but later edited out of the movie.

Nothing has changed in this respect and the retelling of the Wallace story through *Braveheart* elicits much the same response. Visiting Lanercost in Northern England and the Wallace Monument in Stirling, Scotland you discover two very different pictures of the same man. It depends of course which side you are on.

Wallace rose up, was loved by the people, was feared by those in power, who set about discrediting and destroying him. He was betrayed and offered up for execution. By this action, intended to wipe out Wallace, Edward succeeded in making his story live on in people's hearts and minds.

Braveheart appeared in cinemas and was enjoyed by cinemagoers. At the same time, its critics – historical, media and political – were determined to discredit the film.

Among those who have chronicled Wallace's fame, Harry the blind Minstrel is pre-eminent in having devoted his whole force to the glorifying of his hero. Written down two hundred years after Wallace's martyrdom at Smithfield in London, Harry's epic tale of Wallace was addressed to commonalty and great men alike. It is Blind Harry's tale of Wallace that was recreated in Randall Wallace's screenplay *Braveheart*. Randall says: 'Just as Wallace addressed his army in *Braveheart*, so too did Blind Harry's Wallace stand on the field of battle at Stirling and say something which caused his men to wish to stand with him against overwhelming odds.'

Braveheart, the movie, impacted on Scotland and the world with a force as mysterious and contentious as Wallace himself. For Scots it reminded them of what they once were, what they are now and what they yet might be. To the world it gave back the hero, once upheld as the first freedom fighter, revered by many who came after him.

> Definitely go to Stirling, go to the Wallace Monument, see the battlefield from atop the Monument. I could go on and on. My point about going to Scotland and being in Stirling has not only enhanced my feeling for this movie but also brought history leaping from the past and makes it a real experience. Now when I watch the movie, I've been there. I see what they saw, I hear what they heard. The past and my heritage is alive within me.
> Fred Clarke

The response to the movie was the response to Wallace, loved and feared in equal measure. To the people who went in their droves to see the movie, not once but many times, *Braveheart* symbolised the eternal need to fight oppression, to be true to one's heart, to never give up.

[3] 'Most of us, well, we don't live like a man is supposed to live: with passion and honour and integrity and loyalty. We're too busy trying to win and acquire, get and have. It's all about doing what is right. Just what is right.'

The impact of *Braveheart* on Scotland was phenomenal. Despite negative reviews from many critics, *Braveheart* filled the theatres of Scotland from its opening in September 1995 until the following May 1996. Acres of newspaper print were devoted to the discussion of *Braveheart*, Wallace and Scottish history. The great empty well that has been the average Scot's knowledge of their own history was demanding to be filled. *Braveheart* has been responsible for saving Scotland from its own ignorance, not in telling us the truth about Wallace, but in telling us how little we know of our own history.

> *My boyfriend's grandmother is Scottish. She is 85 years old. After we had been to see this movie, I went and asked her about William Wallace. Her face lit up like a child and she told us the story as she was told. Many thanks to Mel Gibson for making her memories come alive again.*
>
> Debbie (South Africa)

The international impact of the film was also enormous, for the story of Wallace and his fight for freedom is universal. *Braveheart* as an epic movie had all the right ingredients for a world looking for a hero. In America it was celebrated with five Oscars, against all the odds. It became a wake up call for all those Americans who were aware their roots were Scottish and now sought to re-establish these roots. It reminded Americans of their own freedom, hard fought for, but sometimes forgotten. Hugely popular in Europe, it reminded people there of their own freedom fighters. In politically oppressive regimes in other parts of the world it gave rise to courage and fortitude and hope.

> *I'm Brazilian, and I live in São Paulo.*
>
> *I have seen Braveheart about 10 times, because this movie use to help me to keep my strength and my ideals alive.*
>
> *The first time I saw the film I was very depressive because I was alone and had to fight every day to survive in a country where the injustice commands, and common people don't have any assistance from the government.*
>
> *Yes, the image of paradise we sell to the foreigners, such as the beautiful beaches and Carnival, don't reveal the global (and desperate) situation of Brazil.*

So, I feel a deep identification with Braveheart concerning the fight of poor people for a new life.

I would like to thank to Mr. Gibson, because his work affected me in such a way, that I can recover my strength to believe in something better.

I love Braveheart!!!

Silvana Camillo Azzelli

Braveheart was a sweeping movie, affecting people politically in Scotland and around the world. But that was not all it was. *Braveheart*, more than anything, was a tribute to a great man, whose story affected individuals deeply. Using *Braveheart*'s image of William Wallace's courage and integrity, individuals throughout the world found courage to face up to personal hardship. This book is – in some small part – a testament to these people, who having found *Braveheart*, found courage.

Since seeing Braveheart we have lost three more babies, two midway in the pregnancy, like our first child was. And, if not for God and the memories of the strength portrayed by William Wallace in Braveheart, I would not have survived this.

As another person said about the movie, whenever I need support for my troubles, which are above the average, I call on my Braveheart strength to see me through . . .

Annette

It is also an attempt to tell the true story of *Braveheart*'s conception, development and success, and the camaraderie and passion it generated among those who took part in it and those who watched it. And also to show how one man's courage, having saved Scotland from oblivion seven centuries ago, played a part in Scotland's democratic future.

Braveheart opened in the United States in the summer of 1995, catching one Scot, a history graduate, unawares.

[4] 'I was ashamed. Ashamed that it was in USA that I'd first heard the inspiring tale of William Wallace. Determined to find out more, I delved into some historical biographies when I returned to Scotland. What surprised me was not *Braveheart*'s occasional departures

from the historical storyline, but the extent to which the film portrayed the real life of William Wallace, even to the point of detail . . . Beware the 'this is fiction' brigade with their synthetic concerns about accuracy. Their Scotland had killed off William Wallace a second time by burying him in the footnotes of history. *Braveheart* brought him back to life.'

Anger and frustration, *Braveheart* caused both in large measure. It also caused elation. When the film was shown in cinemas throughout Scotland, people stood up and cheered. Leaving the cinema, people were already asking the same question. Why were they never told in school about William Wallace?

> My father and I saw this film when it was first released and we both felt a deep sense of pride in how the film depicted us Scots then.
>
> However my father sadly died early February 1996 and my mother at the time said that my father was a true 'Braveheart' and he was buried with his Braveheart jumper on. Sadly my mother passed away only two weeks after burying my father, we scattered their ashes in the harbour at Anstruther so they could be together as long as the seas flow.
>
> I watch the film each year and it still brings back the memories of my father and mother and each year I enter a memorium into the local Falkirk Herald remembering my Braveheart.
>
> Sorry this note is a sad one but it brings happiness to our family when we think of our parents and how they loved Scotland but most of all how they both now have their 'FREEDOM'. We as a nation should always remember what our ancestors and parents fought for and not give it up so easily.
>
> David Machen

As people flocked to see this movie, the backlash against *Braveheart* and Wallace began. The critics' obsession with discrediting *Braveheart* seemed equal to the enthusiasm of the public for both the movie and the resurgence of the Wallace story. Reviled by the majority of historians and media critics, accused of all manner of horrors from xenophobia to homophobia, the strength of reaction against *Braveheart* was steadfastly refuted by those ordinary cinemagoers who saw the movie's true worth. Now many years later *Braveheart* has taken its rightful and positive place in the

Scottish psyche. Culturally and politically the most significant film of the nineties, the time has come to reflect on and celebrate the *Braveheart* Phenomenon.

> *Four years since it was released and many good films later, Braveheart remains the gold standard by which all other films are measured. It is simply the most gut-wrenching film ever made.*
>
> *I've compared every film I've seen since its release and can honestly say no other film compares.*
>
> *Please note the following: when Braveheart was released, my wife and I managed to steal a night out, away from the kids, house, etc... We didn't go to the theater expecting much and we were not prepared for what we witnessed that night.*
>
> *Throughout the film the audience was visibly shaken. I think it caught many people by surprise, tears seemed to flow at key moments during the film. Near the end, I thought for sure Wallace would be saved. He wasn't. After the closing credits, the lights went on. I will never forget what happened next: NO ONE MOVED. The people sat there, stunned, some in tears, staring at the screen.*
>
> *Jim Lauricella*

Many people who went to watch *Braveheart* could not understand why the movie caused so much angst in Scotland and the UK. Wallace seemed to them a perfect hero. Why all the fuss about the film? The international success of *Braveheart* proved its worth and power as a movie. In Scotland *Braveheart* was much more than that. Struggling with a democratic deficit within an increasingly centralised UK, Scotland seemed powerless to exercise its political, social and cultural beliefs. During Mrs Thatcher's reign of power, Scotland became an increasingly demoralised and depressed nation. The return of the Conservatives in 1992 brought no relief, fighting as they did on the Unionist platform. The new Prime Minister, John Major, said devolution 'was one of the most dangerous policies ever to be put before the British people'. It seemed Scotland was to remain a stateless nation, with little to no say in its present or its future.

Into this time and place the Wallace story re-emerged, creating increased self-confidence in Scotland and spotlighting the issue of self-determination. In 1997 Scotland and the rest of the UK went to the polls. The general election results left not one Conservative Member of Parliament in Scotland. Labour was back in power and devolution was on the agenda.

> I've been a movie buff for most of my life as well as fascinated with Scotland. I'm also a history buff as well. When I saw the movie Braveheart in May 1995, I knew I had seen a magnificent film. I knew then that it would win the Academy Award for the best film. I had never heard of William Wallace; I was taken by his story, so started reading what I could find about him in the States. I had always wanted to go to Scotland, but now I knew I had to, and what I wanted to see.
>
> Bob Reece

Two years after the *Braveheart* premiere in Stirling, on the seven hundredth anniversary of the Battle of Stirling Bridge – Wallace's greatest victory over the invading forces of the English – the Scots voted Yes in the Devolution Referendum of 11 September 1997. On that same weekend around two hundred people arrived in Stirling from all over the world to recognise and celebrate the significant impact the retelling of the Wallace story through *Braveheart* had made on their own lives and on the future of Scotland. Many people associated with the making of the movie attended the *Braveheart* Convention, including Randall Wallace, the screenwriter, and his father.

In 1995 the people of Scotland needed reminding that they could change things, despite the evidence of the previous twenty years. *Braveheart* played its part in changing Scotland. It helped change Scotland's perception of itself and the world's perception of Scotland. For better or worse, Wallace was back.

Chapter Two

Wallace goes to Hollywood

'**W**hen I decided to write about William Wallace I studied . . .
I went to the Library in Los Angeles where I live and tried
to look him up and the *Encyclopaedia Britannica* gives a small
entry about William Wallace. And basically they say that nothing
is known, that there is very little that could be said with certainty
about him. I can tell you honestly that it doesn't make a whole lot
of difference to me. What was obvious in the story was that this
man who had no claim to nobility, rallied the armies of Scotland. He
stood in front of several thousand Scots, outnumbered enormously,
and he said something, which caused them to stand their ground.'

Then Randall had a stroke of luck or fate played its hand. A
young man at the Library in Los Angeles phoned him and told
Randall he had found a book, but it was in deep storage, which
meant it was about to be thrown out. It would take him a couple of
weeks to get it.

'Two weeks later he came to my house and he had a book. It
was a 1722 copy of the reprint of Blind Harry's poem. The book
was 270 years old and they were going to throw it away. I read
that book and my hands shook. It was Blind Harry's story of William
Wallace. Now I had already written a great deal of the story. In fact
I had already written several versions of *Braveheart*, but from that
book I got incidents that made William Wallace really real for me.
For instance, when he goes into the tent and the Princess offers
him a bribe and he tells her that that he won't take the money. And
she asked him why and he tells her how the woman he loved was
killed and then she weeps and asks him to take the money anyway.
That was in *Blind Harry*. Is *Blind Harry* true? I don't know. I
know that it spoke to my heart and that's what matters to me, that
it spoke to my heart.'

Randall Wallace
BRAVEHEART CONVENTION, STIRLING, SEPT 1997

Randall Wallace was eight years old when a cousin came back from holiday in Scotland and told the family that there had been a famous Wallace who had statues raised to him there. The boy Randall was fascinated by his cousin's story. He had never thought of his name being Scottish. He had just assumed it was an American name.

Many years later –

'My wife and I were in Edinburgh and we walked into the castle and saw the statue of William Wallace and I thought, this is a Wallace, a famous Wallace and I'd never heard of him and I asked one of the guards who he was and he said well, he's our greatest hero and I began to read about him, but the actual facts on William Wallace's life as established by historians are minuscule. It's kind of sketchy but luckily there is also a lot of legend that surrounds the character. Those legends gave me a window into who the man truly was, how he had felt about his country. Who he had loved, how he had loved.'

Finding *Blind Harry* gave Randall an insight into the spirit of Wallace. Finding the Wallace Clan Trust convinced Randall that the spirit of Wallace still existed in the Scotland of the present day. Randall pays tribute to the help he received from Seoras Wallace and the Clan Trust.

'We had no resources of our own. They offered us all the resources they had to help us make this movie. And I think if there is a debt that Scotland owes to anyone it is not to me but to them, in that they have carried the spirit down through the years.'

> *OK. It's wonderful entertainment. I have never been so moved by a film. The sheer spectacle, scope and exhilaration of this movie gave me goose-bumps. As Mel said, there is a William Wallace born every century who believes in courage and honour. How can you get complete historical accuracy so far back and who cares? It is the spirit of the man and what he stood for and how he felt. The film should have got 10 Oscars and one more for Mel Gibson's acting. Who else could have portrayed Wallace with such magnetism. Brilliant.*
> *Linda*

Mel Gibson received the script to consider as an actor but it was soon more than that to him.

[5] 'I felt like I had to tell the story all of a sudden, because I kept reworking scenes in my head. It's a good indication that you should direct if you're building the images and sequences in your head. The script was a very haunting piece of work. It wasn't predictable and just the sheer size of it and it's just a funny corner of history that I had never heard of before. It's based on a character called William Wallace who did exist in the 13th century in Scotland. He was a commoner. He was also a patriot. He was actually successful in defeating the English. Wallace was truly interested in liberty and loved his country and he really just wanted to be free. And he wanted freedom for his fellows. But at the same time he was kind of a savage. This is the dichotomy of the man.'

Randall's screenplay had the Scottish nobles dressed in all their finery like the English nobles. The Hollywood backers wanted tartan.

When the Apollo spacecraft landed on the moon, Allan Bean, one of the crew, reverentially laid a swatch of MacBean tartan on the moon's surface. Tartan is a symbol of kinship and belonging, a badge of identity all over the world, which is why it was used in *Braveheart.*

So Randall was called to meet Mel for breakfast to discuss the script. To Randall, a practising Baptist, *Braveheart* had become 'a sermon I preach myself'. Before he went to the meeting, he walked up and down praying that when he met with Mel he would not tell Mel what he might want to hear but rather what he, Randall wanted to say about this story. Randall fully understood the way of Hollywood and how big a risk Mel would have to take with *Braveheart*. Randall said,

'Every movie has a message. Sometimes it's biggest biceps or greenest money that prevails. *Braveheart* says if you are faithful to your heart, to yourself, to what you truly believe, they can cut out your heart and you will still prevail, and not just in the next life, but in this one. It doesn't mean you won't sacrifice everything you have, but in that sacrifice, you will get everything you have.'

The spirituality of *Braveheart* contributed in large part to the movie's impact and Mel was not afraid of that aspect of the script. Randall believed that Mel was a man of a deep spirituality and he was tremendously gratified that Mel, rather than being afraid of the faith that is expressed in this movie, clearly saw that this was something to be fully embraced and brought his own passion to it. As Randall says, Mel delivered the prayers as a man who knows how to get down on his knees and pray.

Charles Knode was nominated for an Oscar for best achievement in costume design. When trying to come up with a suitable tartan, he is said to have found an old pair of tweed trousers at Shepperton Studios. He sent them to the Islay Woollen Mill and asked if they could make a tartan like that. That's why the plaids of the various clans were made from tweed rather than normal tartan cloth.

So somehow in the strange world that is Hollywood, a movie as unusual as *Braveheart* begins to come to life. Mel Gibson is drawn to the script by its epic proportions and haunting quality. Now he must raise the money and make the dream that is *Braveheart* become a reality.

Making *Braveheart* takes a year of Gibson's life.

[6] 'Live, eat, breathe, sleep this story and the telling of it. It's like being dropped in the middle of an ocean and looking around and there's nothing but water but you figure well there's got to be land. I think I'll go that way and it's just one stroke at a time. I had to get up earlier than everyone really to get all dolled up and get ready for the task ahead. I was hopping in front of the camera doing it as best I could. If it wasn't a total disgrace, I might do another one for safety then get to hell on. Because I was so focussed on the story telling and all the other aspects of the whole thing it brought a relaxation to the whole thing because I simply didn't have the energy left to be tense with.'

Gibson chooses his actors by getting to know them.

'*Braveheart* is a very human story about real people. There's real characters on the page and it was my job to strive to make those characters even more real. So I was casting this thing for months. And I didn't read anyone. You know people read people and I don't think that's any use. So what I used to do was to sit down and talk to them for fifteen minutes and you can tell.'

Everyone I spoke to who worked on *Braveheart* talked in the same way about the film. They remembered the atmosphere, the camaraderie, the passion, the fun.

Catherine McCormack reports the first day as being tense for her, worried as she is about the size of the budget. But Mel turns out to be the nicest guy, really down to earth. When they do a scene together they just feel their way through it and run with the script.

There was a bridge in Randall's screenplay of the movie. For various reasons it didn't reach the final film. (see text)

And all the time it rains. Not the real teeming kind of rain but the kind of rain that always drizzles and never stops. It doesn't stop the shooting. Randall gets phone calls telling him the conditions are horrendous but it doesn't matter because it all looks wonderful. They discover Glen Nevis, where they are filming, is the rainiest spot in western Europe. Everyone gets covered in mud. It creates a look they would not have had if the weather hadn't designed it for them.

The logistics of the project are enormous. Gibson wanted to direct an epic and *Braveheart* is an epic, an epic that has two huge battles central to the story. They spend six weeks on the Battle of Stirling with eight cameras and thousands of extras not to mention the horses.

He wants to make this picture move all the time. He watches all the battle movies he can lay his hands on to see the kind of territory that has been covered before and see if he can go further with it and really try to get the feeling of what it must be like to be in the middle of a 13th century battle. He wants to get the smell of it.

They realise early on that they're going to need a large number of disciplined extras and the reserve Irish Army is able to provide this. Hence the move to Ireland. Much has been made of the attraction of Irish tax incentives to the film industry. Gibson maintains that having a disciplined force available in Ireland was the key reason for the move.

Robert the Bruce's brother Edward became High King of Ireland. He died close to the Curagh where the battle scenes for *Braveheart* were shot.

Every day, what they call *The Battle Plan* goes into action. Companies of fifty men march into the camp in combat gear singing. They move from one tent to another. First stop wardrobe, where they change into plaids and battle gear. Next tent, it's war-paint and dirt. Next tent the boys get the battle toys. A couple of thousand people are involved, all with just one vision in mind.

During the Battle of Stirling they do something that's never been done before. They bare a thousand backsides to the camera at the same time.

Mel liked that: [8] 'That's got to be in the *Guinness Book of Records*. 1,000 bare asses on screen in one shot. And that is accurate. The Scots used to lift their kilts and flash the other side. It used to freak the other side out.'

Mel Gibson's middle name is Columcille (Gaelic for St Columba)

The military brilliance and inventive genius of Wallace is highlighted throughout the film. He is an instinctive battle commander and he can stand his ground with his men on the battlefield. Wallace was one of the first commanders to counter heavy horse with the use of the schiltron, which consists of wooden spears grouped together like a porcupine.

[9] 'Because Wallace was a man of the people and he had a real vision for what the country could be and his men loved him. They'd follow him into hell.'

And the battles are hell, choreographed to the finest detail, worked in storyboards, hand to hand combat decided move by move. Mel achieves what he wants, real battle scenes without injury to his actors or the horses. The mechanical horses that take the injuries in the film are made from foam on a metal frame. They each weigh 250lbs.

There were more scenes written with young William and young Hamish than reached the final movie. In some of these they spoke Gaelic together.

$100,000 a horse, $40,000 for the track. The first time this had been done in a movie.

But at the end of the day special effects don't make a movie, characters do. *Braveheart* is full of strong and complex characters, none stronger or more complex than Wallace himself.

This story of William Wallace, myth or reality, is a story of epic proportions. A life without compromise. A life lived in pursuit of a dream. A death filled with hate. An execution ordered by a King who despised Wallace and hoped by destroying him to destroy what he inspired in others.

[10] 'I think Mel's made a terrific film. It's a wonderful story and I can't believe that no one's written a story about this man before because he's just such a passionate person. I think it's important that people know about this man.' (Catherine McCormack, Murron)

[11] 'I hope they can't talk at the end of it. I hope that they're so moved and so inspired by it. That's all. They've watched this great story and they've found something in themselves.' (Mel Gibson)

Mel Gibson's wish came true. When *Braveheart* opened in cinemas something extraordinary happened at the end of each performance. Some audiences cheered. Some cried. But afterwards nobody moved. People sat there in silence listening to the music, watching the credits roll up, showing their appreciation of having been part of something extraordinary. And that something extraordinary brought the audiences back again and again.

Braveheart as a Hollywood movie was a resounding success. Confounding some critics, it was reported to have taken $175 million worldwide by the 5 March 1996 issue of the *Hollywood Reporter*, which ran a special congratulatory issue for Mel Gibson, for achieving 1996 NATO/ShoWest Director of the Year. After achieving success in the Golden Globe awards, *Braveheart* went on to be nominated for ten Oscars in the 68th Annual Academy Awards. It won five; for Best Film, Best Director, Best Cinematography, Best Sound Effects Editing, and Best Make-up.

After the Golden Globe awards, the MacBraveHeart webpages were busy with fans hoping for success at the Oscars, while accepting that *Braveheart* was not a typical Oscar candidate. *Braveheart*'s main competition was *Apollo 13*, a significant movie about the American conquest of space. The British press was suggesting *Sense and Sensibility* should take the honours. But *Braveheart* was the Best Picture winner. A little known Scottish hero, who had inspired the world, inspired the panel of judges.

One of the most harrowing scenes for actors was the killing of Murron. Instinct made everyone want to try and save her.

Those who discussed the film on the Internet, thought *Braveheart* was an awe-inspiring attempt at an epic movie. Many US film critics were amazed that Hollywood had had the guts to finance such a film.

[12] 'Quite simply, *Braveheart* is by a wide margin the best film thus far this year, and the reason is that actor/director Mel Gibson started with a clear vision and carried it through with amazing resolve.'

In *Braveheart*, the written-in-stone law that summer movies must be zany comedies, action flicks with lots of explosions or Disney was confounded. The film's length was a serious oddity in an age of 'get them in, get them out' mentality. Mel could have coasted along for the rest of his career. Instead he chose to make a film so unformulaic that it has critics scrambling to find comparisons.

[13] '*Braveheart* is, predictably, historically suspect, but it is to the film's benefit, that Gibson plays up the legend at the expense of accuracy (but never realism). He dares you to lose yourself in a world of breathtaking beauty, resonating brutality and rip-roaringly good storytelling.'

> *I was against Braveheart when it initially came out, bashed it when it won multiple Oscars at the Academy Awards.*
>
> *Then last year, network television was showing Braveheart in two parts and I balked yet again. What was the big deal with this movie!*
>
> *Then on night two of the broadcast, I caught the last 20 minutes or so. I was immediately sucked into it. I was mesmerized by it.*
>
> *When it was over, I ran to the video store the next day and rented it. Words cannot even describe how much this movie moved me.*
>
> *The romance, the betrayal, man's inhumanity to man, the loyalty, the whole concept of freedom. I absolutely loved it and tried to convince everyone I knew to watch it. I have watched it several times and purchased the movie soon thereafter. I cannot believe I was so blind in the beginning when it first came out.*
>
> Erica Jiggins

The perceived political incorrectness of the film, which was an issue more obvious in American discussions, is also tackled.

[14] 'Much has been made of a scene where Longshanks disposes of his effeminate son's lover. Jeez, lighten up folks. Political correctness wasn't around in those days. Besides it shows something that our society has progressed to the point where such a scene would add to our hatred of the evil king, rather than provide a snicker, as it probably would have not long ago.'

The epic aspects of *Braveheart* were likened to *Spartacus* and *El Cid*, movies Gibson says he saw and admired as a boy.

[15] '*Braveheart* fits comfortably alongside *Lawrence of Arabia* and *Spartacus*; another film to which it favourably compares.'

I've only seen Braveheart once. However, that once had an impact that few other films have ever done.

A couple of days before the Oscar Awards I was listening to a local radio station that was conducting a call-in program about the nominees. The guests on the program were a film instructor and a local film critic. They dismissed Braveheart as a 'male melodrama' and said it would be a 'tragedy' if it won the best movie Oscar. The final indignity was when one of them misquoted Mel Gibson's final line in the movie (she thought he had cried out 'liberty'). I'm not the type to call a call-in show, but I felt someone had to respond. I tried to explain that for someone of my heritage it was a sorely needed expression of cultural origins, and that it if they couldn't even get the final line of 'freedom' right, they may have missed the point.

Later on in the show, as I kept listening, they dismissed my comments as coming purely from my Celtic heritage, that I was seeing the movie from a personal point of view (isn't that what we're supposed to do?). When the Oscar was announced for best film, it was a great moment.

Eric Frazier

The general feeling among American reviewers of the film was that they wanted to hedge their bets. *Braveheart* came out, it was significantly different and no one knew exactly what would happen. What no one anticipated was the effect the movie would have on the people who went to see it. Neither could they foresee that Mel Gibson had directed a film that would collect five Academy Awards.

The movie began to make a serious impact almost immediately.

Within ten to fifteen minutes after the picture began, I turned to my then girlfriend – who I still love – and said 'Valerie, THIS is a great motion picture. and it was and it is. I believe it will stand the test of time like very few films ever have. I told an eighteen year old grocery clerk today that when she is fifty, people will still watch Braveheart with respect and awe. Because it speaks to eternal existential questions that men and women will ponder and struggle to answer as long as the human race exists. God bless Randall Wallace and Mel Gibson for a truly transcending and wonderful film. It may well be the greatest ever made.

Arthur Dresdale

In the UK, *Braveheart* became the fifth biggest grossing movie of
1995. Scotland provided 28% of its national audience, where its
usual share of the market would average 8%. The rest of the UK
comprised 72% of its audience and *Braveheart* was still showing in
England in the spring of 1996 despite the perception that *Braveheart*
was not well received in England. When the British Academy awards
arrived, the panel of judges awarded the prize of best film to *The
Madness of King George*. However when the public vote was
announced, the people of the UK had voted overwhelmingly for
Braveheart as their favourite film.

> I live in Brighton, East Sussex, and Braveheart is a very special movie to
> me on several different levels. As a film, it is excellent – epic in scale but
> personal enough to reach the raw emotions. Beautiful, tragic, dramatic
> and, in many ways, uplifting. I first enountered the film when I heard that
> Mel Gibson was filming it on location. When the film was finally released,
> I went to see it at my local Odeon (largest screen available) despite Barry
> Norman's reservations about the film. I left that cinema shaken. Shortly
> after, I won a copy of the rental video in a contest, and can say that I've
> watched the film countless times - and each time the effect is the same.
> Paul A. Pearson

Braveheart had a similar impact all over the world. Europe, the
Far East, China, Australia, New Zealand, Russia, South America
– the MacBraveHeart web pages have been contacted from all
these countries and more.

> I remember going to watch Braveheart when it first came out in theatres
> here in Canada. I wasn't sure what to expect as I'd seen or heard very
> little about the movie. I am grateful to have seen such a great movie that
> is so inspiring. I have watched the movie more than a hundred times since
> then and will probably continue to watch it as long as I shall live ...
> I am 33 years old and of First Nations/Scottish decent.
> I get a lot of ribbing from my friends and co-workers about my obsession
> with Braveheart which I don't really care ... the history, the music score
> are just so amazingly done ... I have the soundtrack in my car, at my
> office, and listening to the CD is almost like watching the movie again ...

One of the scenes that really gripped me was when they were bringing back young William's father and brother after getting killed. My mother died recently, and seeing how young William reacted was the same way I felt when my boss came to tell me I have to go home for an emergency, I knew instantly that something was wrong and I felt that William knew as well. Scenes such as that make great movies as they grip your true feelings deep inside . . .

I have been to 3rd world countries where oppression is very real and I can relate to what has happened in the history of Scotland and their fight for freedom. I tell you it will give you a very different perception on life when visiting a country where oppression is rampant. Many of us don't realize what has had to be done to get us to where we are today. Could you imagine what it would be like now if 'William Wallace' was never born? Much different I would think. I know for one I wouldn't be here typing my thoughts on this. Like the words at the beginning of the movie say 'History is written by those who have hanged heroes'. There is a lot of misinformation on the teaching of history and past events . . . Braveheart helped me learn a lot about the true history of Scotland which I would have never really learned or found out about anywhere else.

Barney Stirling

Speaking on Scottish Connection on 12 January 1999, Dr Graham Norton of Edinburgh University said [16] 'Since *Braveheart*, we have seen a renaissance in Scottish history. This renaissance has an international dimension. Postgraduate courses have shown the biggest growth with European students predominant. *Braveheart* has taken Scottish history onto a level of popular consciousness that has been missing for some time.'

Wonderful story and wonderful film too.

Is it exaggerated? Maybe. Is it not completely faithful to history? Probably. But WHO CARES?

Josepth Andrew Amoros from Catalonia

Through the power of Randall's pen and Mel Gibson's film-making passion, the Wallace legend becomes a dramatic reality for millions around the world. Some watch this great story and find something in themselves, as both Mel and Randall hoped for. For others in Scotland and around the world, watching *Braveheart* raises awareness of their Scottish past. Yet others find *Braveheart* heightens their interest in Scottish history and sets them on the path to finding out more.

> *Powerful, moving, inspiring, motivating, encouraging, magnificent, wonderful, simply the best motion picture ever made in the history of the world.*
> Michael Delaney

> *I had to write and testify that Braveheart stunned my soul and captivated my senses. The movie lays out an unadulterated portrait of courage that is hard to ignore.*
> Jason Williams

> *I saw Braveheart twice within the first few days it came out. I didn't know if my boyfriend realized the impact the movie had on me, until the next day at work when a florist showed up with a huge bouquet of wildflowers, with a note that read, 'I tried to locate a Scottish thistle but had no luck. I hope these will do.' I just lost it. I'm very proud of my Scottish heritage, this movie made me feel that I have a part of this history inside of me always.*
> Kim Lodato

> *I went to see Braveheart for the fourth time yesterday. I have never been so moved by a single movie in my life. It's nice to see that people actually like well made movies, in an age of Hollywood garbage.*
> Seering

Chapter Three

Let Battle Commence

What is the historical basis of *Braveheart*? This is a question I'm asked often. Probably the most aggressive way that question was ever put to me was by a journalist from London, who called me with great anger in his voice and said, 'Mr Wallace, what do you consider your responsibilities as a historian,' and I said 'none. I am a dramatist. If you want to argue about whether a piece of drama is accurate in every detail then go pick at Shakespeare.' He said, 'yes Mr Wallace, but you have made it seem that the current British Royal Family is directly descended from William Wallace.' And I said, 'I want to apologise publicly for that. It was never my intention to insult the memory of William Wallace.

Randall Wallace
BRAVEHEART CONVENTION, STIRLING, SEPTEMBER 1997

nitially, *Braveheart* caught the imagination of the critics. Although they mentioned historical inaccuracies, much of the concern seemed rooted in the cheeky idea of Hollywood making a movie about Scottish history. As *Braveheart* gripped the popular imagination, a series of articles began to emerge from a small group of media and history academics slating *Braveheart* in the language of these disciplines. *Braveheart* was accused of being historically inaccurate. People who went to see *Braveheart* were accused of being crazed anglophobes, xenophobes, vulgar and interested in the pornography of torture.

In Scotland, the most widely discussed fault centred on historical accuracy. The critics accused Mel Gibson and Randall Wallace of messing with our history. In answer to the historical criticism, letters abounded in the media from Scots who had never been taught any Scottish history and had little knowledge of their national hero before *Braveheart*. People were annoyed, not that *Braveheart* messed with their history, but that they had been taught so little.

Despite arguments against the historical accuracy of *Braveheart*, no one seemed aware that the script of *Braveheart* borrowed extensively from *Blind Harry's Wallace*. Blind Harry or Harry the Minstrel is thought to have lived between 1440 and 1493. His one major achievement was to gather and record stories of Wallace. Until *Braveheart*, *Blind Harry's Wallace* was only available in expensive academic editions, despite being the most commonly owned book in Scotland next to the Bible, for several hundred years following its translation by William Hamilton of Gilbertfield in 1722.

Blind Harry's Wallace was the inspiration for many works, including Robert Burns' song *Scots Wha Hae*. This major work on Scotland's national hero was unknown and unavailable to the majority of Scots until after the success of *Braveheart*. Then Elspeth King, Curator of the Stirling Smith Museum, was instrumental in bringing *Blind Harry's Wallace* to the Scottish bestseller charts through its re-publication by Luath Press in 1998.

The image of *Braveheart*'s Wallace was also a source of contention, despite the fact that each painting or statue of Wallace was created in the vision of its time, from the Earl of Buchan's sandstone Goliath standing on a hillside, staring out over the Tweed valley, to the tartan-clad images in the great panorama of the Battle of Bannockburn, painted by Philip Fleischer of Munich in 1889.

We know very little of what Wallace looked like. Only the size of the sword is some indication of the stature and strength of the man. Randall says that Mel Gibson joked with him about playing the part, saying he was too old as well as being too short. Randall replied, 'Mel, I understand your question. But William Wallace stands on the battlefield in front of three thousand Scots outnumbered five to one. And he gets them to stand their ground and fight . . . that's not a job for Tom Cruise!'

Much was also made of the tartanry and blue face paint and how inappropriate this was in a film about a 13th century lowlander. However Braveheart was merely following a long tradition of portraying Wallace in this way, from illustrations in Jane Porter's *The Scottish Chiefs* (1809) to Nigel Tranter's *The Wallace* (1975). As for the blue woad, as Elspeth King points out there is a scene in *Blind Harry's Wallace* where William is visited by the Virgin Mary in a dream and she paints the Saltire on his face.

The manner in which *Braveheart* illuminated a period of Scottish history drove those who saw the film to find out more. It also highlighted the need for Scots to take more care of their history. Visiting the Wallace monument in the 60's, you would have found the famous Wallace sword lying neglected, its case covered with bird droppings. The sword was twice stolen, in attempts to have its plight recognised. Now the story of Wallace has been spread worldwide bringing hundreds of thousands of visitors to Stirling and the National Wallace monument.

Randall brought his father to Scotland to be there on the weekend of Devolution and to attend the *Braveheart* Convention.

The history of Scotland has been and still is, a suppressed history. Most Scots have no collective knowledge of their past. [17] Most Scots are like a man who has lost his memory, groping blindly on, with no idea as to his past.

Thanks to *Braveheart*, the interest in Scottish history has burgeoned, both within Scotland and worldwide. Walk into any bookstore now in Scotland and there is a large section, not only on Scottish history, but Scottish culture, literature and politics. For, contrary to some critics, *Braveheart* has not made Scotland look ridiculous on the world stage, but rather the 'heart' of *Braveheart* has been its strongest ambassador.

Mhairi Calvey who played the young Murron was living on the island of Arran when she was auditioned for the part at her primary school. She came with her mum to the 1997 *Braveheart* convention where she met Randall for the first time. He picked her up and swung her round, delighted to meet the wee girl who had brought his young Murron to life.

There were also a number of academic articles attacking *Braveheart*. Most of these were written in the knee jerk reaction immediately after the film was released. They propounded statements on the dire consequences of *Braveheart*, on the film industry in Scotland, on the people who went to see it. Colin McArthur in the paper *Braveheart and the Scottish Aesthetic Dementia* said, [18] It is as if an aesthetic dementia had gripped the Scots, rendering them blind to the empty populism, the slavering xenophobia, the sheer stylistic vulgarity of *Braveheart*. The movie displays a certain vulgar pictorialism, most gross in the scenes involving Wallace and Murron and Wallace and Isabelle. Scenes are clichéd, pre-existing, crass (as in the thistle scene with the young Murron and William).

The same critic went on to suggest that showing the instruments of torture at the execution scene was indulging in the pornography of torture and likened the narrative to those of certain societies such as the ante-bellum American South and Nazi Germany.

Was McArthur right? Certainly the received messages of the audience as predicted by McArthur and what audiences actually received from the film are dramatically different, as can be seen by the sample of the responses published in this book.

Over ten thousand emails later, the MacBraveHeart website has

I found the scene where young Murron presented young Wallace with a simple gift of a thistle flower as possibly the most touching scene I have ever come across in any movie.

Sam Cheang

one of the most comprehensive group of audience responses ever collected. A systematic study of these responses provides a much more positive outcome for the movie than McArthur could have imagined.

McArthur finishes the article with the suggestion that, now available on video, the showing of *Braveheart* to Scottish football and rugby supporters en route to matches against England will whip them into a frenzy of xenophobia, but subsequently retracted this suggestion after Scottish football fans (the Tartan Army) continued to be cultural ambassadors for Scotland, renowned for their good behaviour.

Braveheart also provided a vehicle for academic argument about historiography and the popular narrative film. By this we mean how closely should a dramatist represent history? Robert McKee, the American guru of screenwriting, voices the opinion that [19] the weakest possible excuse to include anything in a story is, 'but it actually happened.' What happens is fact, not truth. Truth is what we think about what happens.

He is very particular on the subject of historical films. [20] What is past must be present. The only legitimate excuse to set a film in the past and thereby add untold millions to the budget, is an anachronism – to use the past as a clear glass through which you show us the present.

Critics argued that *Braveheart* did not properly represent thirteenth century Scotland (it failed on the historiography front). Neither, they said, should the film have been seen as culturally significant in Scotland on the threshold of the twenty-first century since it relied on the kailyard and tartanry images of Scotland.

The reason *Braveheart* engaged people in Scotland and around the world appears to be because it related to their present circumstances (as Robert McKee suggested it would have to). And, contrary to McArthur's suggestion that such images, which he calls tartanry and kailyard, 'interpolate Scots with a sense of their own inferiority', the heart of *Braveheart* has strengthened Scots' image of themselves and the international image of them.

Braveheart was arguably the first Internet film. It is the first film to have a large body of evidence collected via the web about it, showing the effect on the individuals who went to see it. What makes the evidence on *Braveheart* even more interesting is its global nature, in addition to the cultural impact in Scotland. Judging by the evidence in this book, the reactions of people to *Braveheart* are more complex and sophisticated than many critics would have us believe. Certainly with hindsight, the dire warnings of the consequences of *Braveheart* have proved to be nonsense. But still such articles are written and go into print. Why? Maybe because bad stories make good copy.

Mel has a reputation for playing jokes and the rest of the cast joined in. In Hamish's father's death scene, Brendan Gleeson (Hamish) looked down to find James Cosmo (his father) wearing a red plastic nose.

The cultural event that McArthur decries is identified less negatively by other analysts. For example Tim Edensor suggests, [21] [The] symbolic importance of Wallace has been given a giant boost by the international and domestic success of the Hollywood blockbuster *Braveheart*.' He also suggests that slotting films about Scotland into the rigid categories that McArthur et al prefer 'ignores the interpretations of audiences, and the ways such representations are reclaimed, recycled and used to express a wide range of meanings.'

Audience response to *Braveheart* was remarkable in the positive attitude and breadth of its feeling. This huge groundswell of popular opinion persisted whatever the establishment chose to say about the film.

Scottish newspaper reviews were an interesting mixture. Over the period of 2–10 September 1995, *Braveheart* was discussed no less than nine times in *The Scotsman*. In the 2 September issue (prior to the European premiere), there was a positive article about the making of the film, together with interviews with Gibson and some of the other actors. By the 3rd September, Allan Massie, historian, novelist, and columnist, was describing *Braveheart* as '[a] travesty of history and a leaden piece of work'. He went on to offend many readers with the following statement; 'No one can doubt that Wallace fought for freedom, and if he showed a callousness amounting to brutality, well it was in a good cause. The fact that Bosnian Serbs may feel the same way about General Mladic need not disturb us here.'

By 4 September Brian Pendleigh was suggesting that we 'forget the history, *Braveheart* is a film for Scots to identify with . . . [It] provides one of Scotland's greatest heroes with a monument as impressive in its own way as the one outside Stirling.'

David O'Hara (Stephen of Ireland) was a Scotsman playing an Irishman. Brendan Gleeson (Hamish) was an Irishman playing a Scotsman. Peter Hanley (Edward's son) was an Irishman playing an Englishman.

In the same edition we were treated to a picture of Mel Gibson at the European premier with the heading, 'feeling great to be Scotland's hero'. However Alan Taylor had 'no wish to wade through Hollywood's vision of Scotland's past.' While Angus Wolfe Murray, on the 8 September, was telling us not to believe the hype, 'Mel Gibson's *Braveheart* is too long, simplistic and rides off in the wrong direction.'

By 10 September, the letters page was fighting back. Ian Black of the Wallace Society suggests, 'Massie knows, political change or none, Scotland is in no danger of the kind of civil war that has consumed Yugoslavia. To hint at such terrors is to let a propagandist enthusiasm overwhelm the artist's integrity.'

Almost immediately, this Hollywood movie about a Scottish hero was becoming a political football. It could be argued that the timing of the movie was the problem, coming as it did in the lead up to a General Election when Devolution was on the cards. But why? William Wallace fought for Scottish Independence seven hundred years ago. Why fear his re-appearance now? The power of a good movie perhaps?

In 1810, Jane Porter's *The Scottish Chiefs*, a best selling book based on *Blind Harry*'s *Wallace,* was translated into Russian, German and French. Napoleon had it banned as a dangerous influence. No one could ban *Braveheart*, although the BBC did slot in its first television broadcast on the Thursday after New Year 1998 thus avoiding the prime viewing time of the festive period when many more people would have seen it. This angered many people in Scotland, seeing this as a political decision on the part of the BBC.

The London press (*The London Evening Standard* and *The Sunday Times*) knew exactly why the film had been scheduled at this time and not over the Christmas period. They pronounced

Braveheart 'a malodorous film. One which has done more than any other to bring about the demise of Britain. A film which has fired the natural Anglophobia of working class Scotland.'

The strength of reaction to *Braveheart*, in whatever direction, positive or negative, is a clear indication of the power of the film. *Braveheart* had somehow managed to hold up a mirror to present day Scotland, rattling political, media and historical cages in the process.

Neal Ascherson echoed many Scots' feelings about *Braveheart* by being moved, slightly embarrassed, proud and worried by the film, all at the same time.

'Seeking heroes, I went the other day to see *Braveheart*. As an account of the real William Wallace, or of late 13th century Scotland, it is a joke. The list of cultural and historical distortions rolls on forever . . . You go to scoff . . . and yet there are moments when this chilling shocker takes you unawares. One strong minded, progressive friend found herself in tears. Another Scottish colleague reacted with a furious attack on the film for reducing his country's struggles to crude anti-English racism. Both went to the film certain they were immune to its allure – but neither was. They saw a child give a flower to a boy standing at his murdered father's grave, and the flower was a thistle. They heard a man speak easily of his country's 'freedom' without seeking a lesser word. Suddenly, they were undone. Wallace is a real hero, which means he lives on in the shadows at the back of people's heads.'

This worry was not echoed by the respected Scottish actor, Ian Bannen, who played the Bruce's father in *Braveheart*. His fax to the *Braveheart* Convention of September 1997 was openly proud;

'Young people's charities tell me that the last two years have seen a huge pride and honour felt by young Scots in their country and their nationality. This is due in very large part to *Braveheart* and to Mel and to Randall. We owe them much gratitude. I am proud to be a Scot and proud to have been part of *Braveheart* – even if I was on the wrong side.'

So who are we to believe? Was *Braveheart* a national embarrassment, a bad film, simply xenophobic or homophobic rantings, historical mishmash, sentimental hogwash, politically unwise, appropriated by sinister forces, indulging in the pornography of torture, full of vulgar pictorialism; or was it a film that spoke to our hearts, that gave us a glimpse of the eternal truths of life, whatever the country or century we live in?

Despite the truism that history is written by the winners, in the war over *Braveheart*, for once the people will have written the final story. Every attack on *Braveheart* has brought a rapid and prolonged response from its audience. There have been countless letters and articles, television programmes and discussions covering all aspects of *Braveheart*. Why has this film caused so much passion? This was not a film of merchandising spin-offs like *Star Wars*. In fact little to no merchandise accompanied the film. It is an old film now by popular standards. It has not achieved cult status. We would argue, based on the accumulated responses of ten years that it is above narrow cult status. *Braveheart* has had a profound effect on the lives, hopes and aspirations of people all over the world.

So why were some critics, particularly in the United Kingdom, so quick to condemn *Braveheart*? It was certainly not the first time historians have ridiculed or tried to ignore the popular Wallace. In a letter to *The Herald* on Thursday 25 February 1999, as the new Museum of Scotland opened, empty of Wallace, Michael Donnelly wrote,

Angus McFadyen (The Bruce) was originally called to audition for Edward's son. Peter Hanley was in line for The Bruce. Angus decided he really wanted to play The Bruce. When he went in to audition he asked outright to audition for The Bruce (with the help of some Dutch courage).

'Hamilton of Gilbertfield's popular translation of 1722 (of *Blind Harry*) had a similar impact on the contemporary population as Mel Gibson's film. Certainly Hamilton's many editions had a profound impact on the political and literary life of Scotland, triggering the conscious renewal of the Wallace cult by the 11th Earl of Buchan and Robert Burns, among others.'

Could this be the reason why *Braveheart* was subjected to such prolonged criticism, not just by film critics but by the establishment en masse? Was it because *Braveheart* had resurrected the cult of Wallace once again and at a time of political upheaval in Scotland, where moves were afoot to bring back a Parliament after three hundred years? Michael Donnelly concluded,

'Historians like TC Smout, Tom Devine and Michael Lynch have as much hope of confining Wallace to a footnote on 'Scottish Trade and the Burghs' as Dr Andrew Noble and his motley crew have of suppressing popular delight in this most enduring of legends.'

Michael Donnelly has been proved correct. The historians who rubbished *Braveheart* have ironically seen their subject benefit dramatically from the film, with an increase in interest in Scottish history at all levels and from all round the world. Contrary to what they suggested, *Braveheart* has proved to be the biggest history lesson ever.

While the arguments raged on all aspects of the film, people continued to flock to see it. *Braveheart* ran in cinemas in Scotland from September 1995 to June 1996. Then the people bought it on video and watched it again and the word *Braveheart* permanently entered our vocabulary.

Brendan Gleeson was a well-known stage and screen actor (and fiddler) in Ireland before *Braveheart*. Mel Gibson auditioned him by going to watch him in a play there.

In early January 2000, Part 10 of the Millennium Commissioned Lottery Project, the magazine *Scotland's Story*, told in weekly parts, reached the newsagents. The front cover pictures William Wallace as portrayed by Mel Gibson in *Braveheart*. Inside there are three more images from the movie being used to illustrate the story of Wallace, the man of the Millennium.

Inside this publication, Professor Ted Cowan re-quotes the same critical paper by critic Colin McArthur about the movie, yet says,

'But the historical detail (of Wallace) is almost a distraction. The strength of the Wallace legend lies in the fighting qualities of the man, and his raw courage in the face of a gory and sadistic death. Wallace's victory at Stirling Bridge gave Scotland back her pride and paved the way for us to be a nation again.'

Chapter Four

Death and Resurrection

I believe the story of William Wallace and who William Wallace truly was and who William Wallace is now, exists because of the people of Scotland. It exists because in this place and among these people . . . and by these people I mean you as well. People who would come here and who would consider the story of *Braveheart* to be something moving and important and lasting and significant. That story of courage and love and loyalty was rooted in the hearts of the people here. I don't mean of everyone but that's the point. The point of the story is that not everyone will be faithful to their heart the way William Wallace was faithful to his. The point too, on this particular occasion when Scotland recognises and the world recognises a level of Scottish Independence . . . is that independence is not something you really achieve at the ballot box, no matter how the vote goes. Freedom is something that you have to live.

Randall Wallace
BRAVEHEART CONVENTION, STIRLING, SEPTEMBER 1997

William Wallace died on the 23 August 1305. The manner of his death shocked commoner and nobility in Scotland alike. [22] A show trial at Westminster, where he was crowned with laurel, was followed by a five-mile journey face down on a hurdle drawn by two horses. True to recorded events, *Braveheart* has Wallace stating he could not be guilty of treason never having sworn allegiance to Edward of England. Wallace was hanged at Smithfield, then disembowelled while still conscious. His entrails were burned. The execution scene in *Braveheart* was kinder to Wallace than Edward I was. It is reported that Wallace, a deeply religious man, asked to look at his Psalter before he died. Wallace's head was put on a spike on London Bridge and his body quartered and the four pieces sent to Newcastle, Berwick, Stirling and Perth to be put on display as a warning to the people of Scotland not to try to thwart Edward's plans for them.

Because Wallace had no burial place, Scots have long chosen to honour places and objects associated with him. Oral tradition played a strong part in this and items associated with him were revered and passed from generation to generation within families. Current OS maps identify over eighty places in Scotland with Wallace.

Blind Harry's Wallace reads like a Wallace tourist guide to Scotland. No other figure in Scotland's history has been so revered. The naming of the landscape of Scotland in this manner was a form of secular canonisation, before the stories came to be written down. William Wordsworth, England's great poet, recognised this in his poem to Wallace.

> . . . I would relate
> How Wallace fought for Scotland; left the name
> Of 'Wallace' to be found like a wild flower
> All over his dear country; left the deeds
> Of Wallace, like a family of ghosts
> To people the steeps rocks and river banks
> Her natural sanctuaries, with a local soul
> Of Independence and stern Liberty.

Although it is suggested by Allan Massie, in his Mladvic article, that the National Wallace monument at Stirling was erected at a time of satisfaction with the Union, that is not the whole story. One of the first formal Wallace monuments was erected in Wallace-stone, near Falkirk in 1810, put up by colliers who identified with Wallace and his cause. The colliers of Scotland, working in the coal mines of the central belt, were kept in serf-like conditions until the late 18th century. They were forbidden to choose their place of work and their sons and daughters were condemned to follow their parents into the mines. The concept of fighting for freedom was one they knew well.

In 1819 magistrates in Paisley jailed a band for playing the song *Scots Wha Hae (Robert Bruce's March to Bannockburn)* at a reform demonstration.

Scots wha hae wi' Wallace bled
Scots wham Bruce has aften led
Welcome to your gory bed
Or to victorie
Now's the day and now's the hour
See the front o' battle lour
See approach proud Edward's power
Chains and slaverie

Wha will be a traitor knave?
Wha can fill a coward's grave?
Wha sae base as be a slave?
Let him turn and flee
Wha for Scotland's King and Law
Freedom's sword will strongly draw
Freeman stand or Freeman fa'
Let him follow me.

By Oppression's woes and pains
By your sons in servile chains
We will drain our dearest veins
But they shall be free

Lay the proud Usurpers low
Tyrants fall in every foe
Liberty's in ever blow
Let us do or die.

This song, written by Robert Burns, asked Scots to take inspiration from the deeds of Wallace and Bruce. Like many other banned songs, *Scots Wha Hae* became an anthem (many Scots today believe it should be the national anthem).

Within weeks, people took to whistling and singing it in defiance. Every August the Sir William Wallace Grand Lodge of Free Colliers commemorate William Wallace, by meeting at the Wallace Stone, where Wallace watched English troops advancing before the Battle of Falkirk.

The majority of the formal Wallace monuments were raised between 1800-1870 both in Scotland and around the world. In 1812 the 11th Earl of Buchan scandalised his class by erecting a Goliath of a monument to Wallace at Dryburgh. The Earl of Buchan was a liberal thinker for his time and ostracised for his views. He supported George Washington and the cause of American Independence. Washington was also an admirer of Wallace and the Earl had a beautiful presentation box made for Washington, 'the Wallace of America' from the ancient Wallace oak in the Torwood near Stirling. Buchan also supported the French Revolution, parliamentary reform and education for women. For this he attracted ridicule and contempt from his contemporaries. Sir Walter Scott said that he wanted to blow up the giant statue of Wallace at Dryburgh to stop it staring out over his land.

Pro Libertate, the Wallace motto, was the masthead of *The Liberator,* a Scottish radical newspaper published in the 1830s. At one time this newspaper rivalled the circulation of the *Glasgow Herald*. It collapsed after the Cotton Spinner's Union was prosecuted in 1838.

By the mid 19th century Wallace was again to the fore, as patriotic leaders such as Garabaldi (1807-1882) and Mazzini (1805-1872) in Italy, Kossuth (1802-1894) in Hungary and Louis Blanc

(1811-1882) in France took inspiration from Wallace and became the Wallaces of their own countries. All these men made contributions to, and wrote letters of support for the erection of the National monument to Wallace in Stirling.

The discomfort with the radical aspects of Wallace was demonstrated by Michael Forsyth, the Conservative Secretary of State for Scotland, when *Braveheart* was released. Following Forsyth's booing by the crowds at the European premiere in Stirling, he suggested it was typical of Scots that they revered someone who failed (Wallace) more than someone who succeeded (Bruce).

It has been the traditional method in the teaching of history to concentrate on kings, queens and dates. The history of ordinary people has generally been viewed as irrelevant. It is only relatively recently that the peoples' history has been championed by some historians.

The oral nature of much of the Wallace story is viewed with suspicion by many historians. Unfortunately, because of the recurring invasions of Scotland by England and subsequent destruction of documents relating to Scotland as a nation, much of the material required by traditional historians has been lost, stolen or destroyed.

On St Andrews Day, 30th November 1998, the £64 million National Museum of Scotland opened to the public. Their interest in Scottish history fuelled by *Braveheart*, they flocked to the new museum in droves. Then they noticed something astonishing. William Wallace was no-where to be found.

A heated debate followed in newspapers and the media concerning the omission of Wallace, and also the limited coverage of other 'anti-establishment' areas of Scottish history such as the Highland Clearances, the ethnic cleansing in the aftermath of the Battle of Culloden, and the part played by the English government in the failure of the Darren Scheme.

In reply to one letter of complaint, the Museum was quoted in *The Herald* on 14 December as saying, 'Our display reflects the material that has survived which sometimes suggests a different version of history from written accounts.'

The arguments went on through January and February 1999.

The feeling was that the National Museum of Scotland did not want 'to do a *Braveheart* thing' by telling the story of Wallace. It was argued that there were no items available to put on display; then the *Scotland on Sunday* newspaper discovered the Lübeck letter after one phone call to Germany. The Lübeck letter was written by Wallace and Andrew de Moray after the Battle of Stirling Bridge, to the merchants of Lübeck in Germany in an attempt to restore trading. This was the letter the Museum director claimed he didn't know existed. He also didn't know about a copy of the letter else-where in the museum, buried in its 'appropriate context' of 'trade and the burghs', a move approved by a number of prominent his-torians. This copy was still in medieval Latin so that visitors were unaware of the sentiments it contained, namely 'Thanks be to God, the kingdom of Scotland has now, by battle been recovered from the power of the English.'

In another section of letters to the *Herald* in January, headed 'The hero has broken loose', one correspondent suggested that critics north and south of the border could argue until they were blue in the face, but the hero they didn't want to tell you about in school, and apparently in the National Museum of Scotland, was now – thanks to *Braveheart* – on the loose all over the world.

> *I saw Braveheart for the first time the other day. By the end I was literally speechless. An incredible story of bravery, loyalty and love. And of course, freedom.*
> Michelle Baker

When the BBC scheduled the first television showing of *Braveheart* for January 1999, controversy raged again. One suggestion was that there had been a conspiracy not to show *Braveheart* at Christmas when everyone was on holiday and would watch it. Others felt it would be irresponsible and inappropriate for the BBC to show *Braveheart* at all, and certainly not until after the May elections to the new Scottish Parliament. Yet the editorial of *The Scotsman* of 19 February, 1999, stated the hard fact that most Scots were astoundingly ill-educated in the history of their country; that the people of Scotland should be remaking their parliament with little or no common knowledge of their past was shameful. 'Future generations should not be denied their heritage in this dismal manner'.

> *Having had a small libation, on the day my son witnessed the opening of a Parliament which I wouldn't have thought likely a few years ago, I felt it was necessary to see if there was anyone on the net with sufficient romanticism about Braveheart to care.*
>
> *I'm delighted to have found your really rather excellent website.*
>
> *Living in Linlithgow, with the palace, and the sense of history that it generates it is impossible not to feel that today was momentous and I curse my employers for not giving us the day off.*
>
> *My apologies for the slightly rambling nature of this email – a mix of William Grant's Family Reserve and the time of night – but I felt that an email of appreciation was in order.*
>
> *Cheers*
>
> *Doug J. 1 July 1999*

In a virtual vote for the *Sunday Herald* on 21 February 1999, the response to the question 'Is *Braveheart* still relevant? was 65% yes. At the same time, the shortlist from which the 100 greatest culturally British films of all time would be chosen was announced. Yet *Braveheart*, the film 'which stirred the heart of the Scottish nation like no other before it . . . and had a massive cultural impact' *(Herald*, 22 February 1999), was left off the list by the selection panel. Dr Andrew Noble, Senior Lecturer in English Studies of the University of Strathclyde was not surprised. He said, 'I would not have any quarrel with it not being on the list. I was sent the script before it was made and fell about laughing. It is Hollywood historical junk.'

But, like it or not, thanks to *Braveheart*, Wallace – as champion of Scotland – was centre-stage again, seven centuries after his death at the hands of Edward I, and at a time when Scotland, a stateless nation, was about to take back her Parliament.

Chapter Five

Universal Truths

Attempting to chart and understand the phenomenon that is *Braveheart*, raises more questions than answers. Why did people love *Braveheart*? Why did so many critics detest *Braveheart*? Why were some people so proud of it? Why were some embarrassed by it? Why did it cause a shiver of fear to run through the establishment in both Scotland and the United Kingdom? Why were endless pages of newsprint dedicated to the discussion of this film (and still are)? Why can't people forget the film? Why is the MacBraveHeart website visited by hundreds of people daily, so many years after the movie's release? Why have the media come to use the term *Braveheart* to symbolise Scotland's admirable qualities? Why have the negative overtones faded over the years? Why are people outside Scotland so moved by this man's story? Why had Scotland, as a nation, forgotten a hero that half the world would gratefully adopt if they could?

Although I am Asian, I am moved by this movie, this man, this story. I can't count the times I have watched this movie, how many times I have read up on William Wallace, how many times I have listened to the soundtrack. It is one of the best movies, if not the best, ever produced.
Charles Nowlin

My name is Wali Bukhari. I am a Shiite Muslim. This is a brave move by Mel Gibson, bringing to the world the history of this brave man, a heart so brave that it makes other hearts brave.

The international perspective on *Braveheart* differs in essence from the Scottish perspective. The English perspective is different again. Cast in the role of aggressors and Wallace's sworn enemies, the film portrayed an aspect of English history that raised questions for many English people. Why did so many people south of the border flock to see *Braveheart* despite the English being portrayed as the bad guys?

The universality of the *Braveheart* appeal helps to answer most of these questions. But how to capture the essence of all the emails, the personal stories from men, women, children; from an infinite variety of colours and creeds, from east and west, north and south? As these emails and stories continue to arrive, three words keep occurring in these messages from around the world and together they seem to reach to the heart of this. As people strive to express the effect this movie has had on them, the words love, courage and freedom appear constantly.

> I just wanted to say that Braveheart was an absolutely fantastic film, probably the best film I have ever seen. May seem strange to hear coming from an Englishman!!! I travel up to Scotland a lot because of my work and I love the country.
>
> Frank Cumming

> My name is Zheng Mian, a Chinese girl. I saw Braveheart on campus. That night is wonderful and unforgettable. I stayed up all that night walking about the campus alone, wondering . . . will I be fighting for something worthy all my life, and I think I will. The movie taught me what I should become.

> You know Braveheart made me fall madly in love with Scotland. The story about William Wallace is so tragic but it makes us reflect on the courage of people we consider as heroes. How they have fought that fiercely is beyond our ability to understand. But the most important part is that I realise that one inspiring person can make a magnificent difference to other people.
>
> Sara Wirjodiardjo

Most movies generate a need to see images from the film. Websites and movie magazines provide these. In the case of *Braveheart* this was not enough. People wanted to express emotion, wanted to tell someone how they felt. Many people saw the film and were moved by the story only to discover to their amazement and delight that such a man did exist.

Despite arguments of authenticity, the basic facts of the Wallace story are the ones that are most important to people. Wallace's father, brother and wife were killed. He rose to defend his country against oppressors and managed against enormous odds to gain time for Scotland. He was betrayed, captured, tried and executed at

The legend begins . . .

WALLACE'S CASTLE, ELDERSLIE.

Undated postcard (likely circa 1900) showing the possible birthplace of
William Wallace in Elderslie. Part of the building was standing until it was
demolished in the 1970s, leaving the footings that are visible today.

(Supplied by Peter Hart)

Statues of Robert the Bruce (left) and William Wallace (right) guard the
entrance to Edinburgh Castle. Randall Wallace visited the castle in 1983,
asked who 'William Wallace' was, and the rest is history . . .

Lin and John Anderson's collection

Monument near Kinghorn, marking the place where, on 19th March 1286, King Alexander III fell to his death, plunging Scotland into a series of succession crises that were to lead to the Wars of Independence.

Lin and John Anderson's collection

Dunfermline Abbey, site of the tomb of King Robert the Bruce.
The spot where the plaque is located below the tree is traditionally believed to be the grave of Wallace's mother.

Lin and John Anderson's collection

'Wallace's Tower' at Airth Castle. Blind Harry's *Wallace* tells how the hero rescued his uncle by storming Airth Castle.

Lin and John Anderson's collection

The Kirk o' the Forest at Selkirk is probably the place where Wallace was knighted, possibly by Sir Robert the Bruce.

Lin and John Anderson's collection

Old St Kentigern's Church, Lanark, where Wallace may have married Marion Braidfute.

Lin and John Anderson's collection

Memorial at Robroyston near Glasgow, marking the spot where Wallace was captured on 3 August, 1305.

Lin and John Anderson's collection

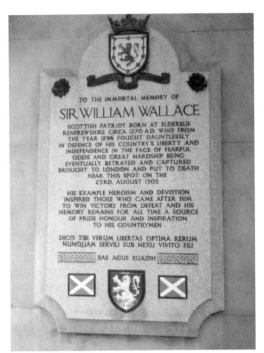

Plaque on the wall of St Bart's Hospital, Smithfield, London, marking the place where William Wallace was executed on 23 August 1305.

Lin and John Anderson's collection

Wallace Stone (in foreground) at Cambuskenneth Abbey, with National Wallace Monument in the distance. Legend has it that the arm of Wallace that was displayed in Stirling after his execution was buried here by the monks of the Abbey.

Lin and John Anderson's collection

Gigantic red sandstone
statue of Wallace at
Dryburgh, erected by the
Earl of Buchan in 1814.

Lin and John Anderson's collection

Wallace Memorial at
Elderslie, erected in 1912
by public subscription.

Lin and John Anderson's collection

Wallace window at Paisley Abbey. It is possible that Wallace as a young man was taught by the monks at the Abbey.

Lin and John Anderson's collection

Tom Church's 'Braveheart' statue at the National Wallace Monument car park.

Susan Hodges

The ANTHONY NOLAN Trust
Taking back lives from leukaemia

Adam Watters dressed as *Braveheart*, a popular tourist attraction at the top of Edinburgh's Royal Mile. Adam has raised several thousand pounds for The Anthony Nolan Trust (Registered charity no. 803716) since 1998. For more information or to make a donation please visit www.anthonynolan.org.uk

The Stone of Destiny, on arrival at Edinburgh Castle on 30 November 1996. Michael Forsyth, Secretary of State for Scotland, is behind the Stone (in kilt). To the right of Mr Forsyth is Alan Stuart, one of the four who liberated the Stone from Westminster Abbey in 1950.

Lin and John Anderson's collection

Cloisters at Bective Abbey, County Meath. Scenes with Princess Isabella, her maid, and Prince Edward were filmed here.
The entrance in the far wall leads into a cell that was used for filming the scene where the Princess visits the condemned Wallace.

Lin and John Anderson's collection

'Lanark' fort and village set in Glen Nevis. Filming had been completed, and the set was being removed (June 1994).

Photo: J Gibson

St John's Castle, Trim, County Meath. Twelve weeks of work in 1994 by the Braveheart crew saw the exterior of the castle transformed into 'York', and the internal courtyard become 'London' (for the execution scene).

Lin and John Anderson's collection

Dunsoughly Castle, County Dublin, was Braveheart's 'Edinburgh Castle'. Its location under the flightpath into Dublin Airport made for difficulties during filming.

St Nicolas Church at Dunsany, County Meath. Built in the 12th century, the ruins were used in 1994 to represent the interior of Westminster Abbey for the wedding of Prince Edward and Princess Isabella in *Braveheart*.

Seoras Wallace, advisor to *Braveheart* and battle crew member,
speaking at the 1997 Braveheart Convention.

Susan Hodges

James Robinson, who played young Wallace in Braveheart, and
Andrew Weir, who played young Hamish at Bannockburn Heritage Centre
(Braveheart Convention, September 1997).

Susan Hodges

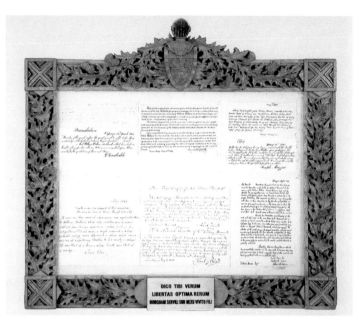

The last remains of the Elderslie Wallace oak frame the letters of support for the building of the National Wallace Monument, sent by Garibaldi and other European patriotic leaders.

Stirling Smith Art Gallery and Museum

Phil Horwood, wearing the Braveheart Warrior tartan, carries the mace presented to the Scottish Parliament by Her Majesty the Queen at the opening of the new parliament building at Holyrood on 9 October 2004.

© Scottish Parliamentary Corporate Body

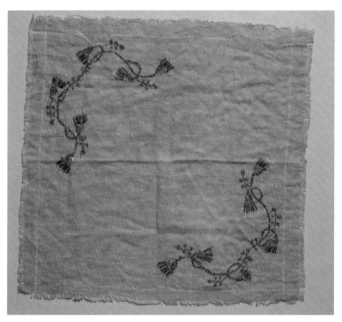

The wedding cloth given to Wallace by Murron in *Braveheart*
(display at Braveheart Convention, August 2000).

The wedding cloth given to Murron by Wallace in *Braveheart*
(display at Braveheart Convention, August 2000).

Randall Wallace,
Braveheart screenwriter,
speaking at the Braveheart
Convention in Stirling
(13 September 1997).
Susan Hodges

Mel Gibson at the
European *Braveheart*
premiere in Stirling on
3 September 1995.
Whylers, Stirling

Steve & Avril Wilson's Braveheart truck
(at Braveheart Convention, August 2000).

Mel Gibson's appearance in the 'Cuddles and Dimples' comic strip in
The Dandy, 16 December 1995, issue no. 2821.

Come South to the Highlands™

The 22nd Annual Central Florida Scottish Highland Games

Seminole Greyhound Park
Casselberry, Seminole County Florida
(Minutes north of Orlando)
SATURDAY, JANUARY 16, 1999

Central Florida Highland Games 1999 brochure, with Chip Crawford (Games organiser) as Braveheart, Ian Hamilton (of Stone of Destiny fame), and Scotty from Star Trek.

Lin and John Anderson's collection

'Keltman' – Braveheart-inspired artwork from Glasgow-based artist and musician Martin Mitchell (1997)

Lin and John Anderson's collection

Smithfield in London and the pieces of his body scattered round the kingdom as a warning. He would not submit to Edward even at the end, though he knew he was the last to resist, the rest having given up, been killed or captured. He must have thought Scotland was finished and that everything he had fought for was gone. Yet by living and dying as he did, true to his heart and beliefs, his inspirational example became the saving of Scotland.

> *I saw Braveheart on opening day here in San Jose, California. After which I ran to the bookstore to find any and all info I could get on William Wallace and Robert the Bruce and to check for literal accuracy in the film. The next evening I went to see the film again. A week later I saw it a third time. I decided if I wanted to continue to be employed and proceed with my wedding plans I would have to NOT spend so much time in the theatre.*
> Christine LoFranco Taylor

Cult films such as *Star Wars* create an imaginary world. Fans of these films fantasise about the world of the film and seek ways of remaining in this world. *Braveheart* has a different effect on people. After seeing *Braveheart*, many have sought the truth about this man and his story, and have held it up as a mirror in which to examine the validity of their own lives and beliefs.

> *This film and the legacy of William Wallace's quest for freedom has had a profound effect on my own life. Perhaps the spirit of Wallace still lives and touches the hearts of people around the world for some inexplicable reason. His story is both wonderful and awful at the same time and evokes such strong emotions that it cannot be forgotten. I will keep the memory of his life in my heart and soul forever.*
> Mary Cole

> *William Wallace was a man who did not let the ideas and beliefs of others influence his own feelings of what was 'right'. I admire William Wallace and not only for his courage, but his strength of conviction.*
> Julie Bachman

Randall Wallace wrote his hero as true, loyal, able to love, unable to be bought. There are extensive parallels with the Christ

Story: in the scene of temptation in the tent, where the Princess offers him money and he angrily asks her, should he be Judas? And later as he goes alone to meet his betrayers as if it is inevitable, and in the prison cell where he prays for the strength to meet his fate. The final execution scene sees him symbolically crucified, all the time being asked to deny his very soul.

> The appeal to me of Braveheart was that in this world where everything seems material, Braveheart reminds us that there are some things that are worth fighting for. To quote the movie 'it's all for nothing if you don't have freedom'.
>
> C Naismith – Australia

Many people who saw the film began questioning where their present day values stood in comparison. What were they striving for in our consumerist society, slaves to work and credit card balances. The people who were affected by *Braveheart* asked themselves questions like this over and over again.

> The movie was the best I had ever seen.
> I was truly touched and inspired by it also. I have seen it so often, and every time I cry. My three favourite parts are:
> The love in his eyes for his wife at the beginning and the joy they share in their love for one another.
> The second part is the look of betrayal in William's eyes on the battlefield when he unmasked Robert.
> The third is at the end when he yells freedom.
> What a movie.
>
> Debra White

The Bruce character in the film represents the majority of us; indecisive, trying to go the way of most gain while still trying to do what is best. The Bruce seemed to symbolise for many the indecision of Scotland then and also the position of Scotland in 1995. How pressed do you have to be before you stand up and fight for what is right? Scots would not lose their lives over constitutional change but there were plenty prophets of doom out there telling them they would lose just about everything else. Bruce wanted to be like Wallace, uncompromising, followed by people because of their love and admiration. His father told him a different truth; that all men lie, all men betray, that is what it takes to be a leader of men.

Over and over again, the responses to *Braveheart* ponder the same concepts and how they relate to our own lives – the meaning of integrity, of loyalty, of love, of honour, of courage, of freedom. The movie's detractors saw none of these. They were like Bruce's father; blind to the soul of his son.

> *Students don't want to learn about history, and movies as brilliant as this one provoke interest in all ages. I am going to get some books on William Wallace. This movie has provoked me to have an interest in the history of people around me, whether I'm Scottish or not.*
> Laurene

In contrast to the critics, people the world over, hungry for Scottish history and the Wallace story in particular, flocked to watch the movie again and again. This audience, free from the professional baggage of the academic, grasped the truth of the story.

> *Braveheart was the movie that celebrated the essence of love, honour and freedom and the strength and courage of character that is needed to possess and cherish these eternal virtues. It is an inspiration of spirit that transcended time and allowed us to hear William Wallace's battle cry.*

In Scotland, *Braveheart* provided (and still provides) [23] a litmus test for political and cultural allegiance at a time of crucial change. This movie has done more to stimulate interest in the culture, politics and history of Scotland than any film before it. The trauma caused by the loss of a major part of the filming of *Braveheart* to Ireland provided the catalyst for changes and improvements to support the Scottish film industry. It has brought people to Scotland 'in droves and hundreds and thousands'. The word *Braveheart* has become synonymous with Scotland.

> *Braveheart is without a doubt the best movie I have ever seen. Mel Gibson has definitely captured the heart in Braveheart.*
> Robinson

When Nelson Mandela addressed the combined Houses of Commons and Lords in the Great Hall of Westminster, he stood where Wallace had stood, when defying his accusers. When told this, Mandela was said to be 'delighted'. He had, of course, 'seen the movie'.

Chapter Six

Braveheart and Belonging

Braveheart was probably the first 'Internet' movie, emerging as it did when email, the web, and web access were sufficiently advanced to allow an audience to celebrate both their sameness (as human beings) and their cultural diversity, online. Those who felt bereft of a culture by the circumstances of their lives found something significant in the culture they saw portrayed in *Braveheart*. Indeed, this was one of the things that worried the critics, wrongly assuming as they did that the movie's culture was one of violence and Anglophobia. In contrast, the world audience saw a culture rich in the motifs of belonging, rooted in geopoetical images of the place of belonging and filled with the motivation to protect that place.

If people feel Scottish, it is surely in a cultural sense. People with long lost ancestral roots feel this as keenly as those who come to live here from elsewhere, enthusiastically adopting Scots culture as their own.

Frederick Douglass, a Negro slave who escaped slavery on a Maryland plantation to become a celebrated author, was a great admirer of Burns. He came to Scotland in 1845 and stayed in Ayrshire, the home area of his hero. Four years later, he was invited to address a Burns Supper in Rochester, New York, where he described Scotland to his listeners as, [24] 'a country where every stream, hill, glen, and valley had been rendered classic by heroic deeds on behalf of freedom. . . . I am not a Scotchman, and have a coloured skin, but if a warm love of Scotch character – a high appreciation of Scotch genius – constitute any qualities of a true Scotch heart, then indeed does a Scotch heart throb beneath these ribs.'

Julie Austin (the young bride) was told to choose her own 'silent' words to her husband before she was taken away by the English nobleman.

I just saw Braveheart last weekend. When my husband and I went, I had only had three and a half hours sleep the previous night and I was afraid that, since the movie was so long, I might be tempted to doze off during it. The film caught my attention in the first few minutes and my eyelids never once thought about drooping! It is men like William Wallace who do what they know to be right no matter what the danger to them, who change the course of history for the better.

Norine Walmsley

[25] Between 1861 and 1931, a total of 960,000 people left Scotland, 680,000 of these from the highlands. At worst these emigrations were forced, at best encouraged. The Highland Clearances cleared people off the land. Many of these emigrant Scots passed on their Scotland-loving genes to their ancestors. This Caledonian diaspora exists in huge numbers around the world. The Irish diaspora was popularised by Mary Robinson during her Irish Presidency. In her inauguration speech, she said she wished to represent those 70 million world-wide who claim Irish descent as well as the 3.5million who live in Ireland now.

Sandy Nelson (William's older brother John) is now a popular Scottish stand-up comedian.

A light is kept burning in Dublin's Phoenix Park as a symbolic sign that these emigrants are cherished. Scotland also lost its heart through countless emigrations of its people. Perhaps Scotland should remember, as Ireland has, just what we have lost.

> *I just happened upon your website and was very pleasantly surprised to see that there are so many who were impacted by Braveheart as much as I have been. I live in Denver, Colorado, USA. I watch Braveheart nearly once a week, and it seems that each time is a new experience. The movie depicts a life that inspires me to live a life filled with faith, courage, and freedom.*
>
> *Scott Rosanbalm*

Braveheart united many people across the globe in a sense of Scottishness, either through the recognisable imagery of Scotland; the music, the voices, the sentiments or, as with Frederick Douglass, showed them 'a country where every stream, hill, glen, and valley had been rendered classic by heroic deeds on behalf of freedom.'

In a *Herald* editorial of Monday 17 May 1999, Scotland the Brand's research into what qualities the international community associated with Scots reported that they are seen as tenacious, spirited, but also nostalgic. 'It may be controversial to mention it, but the *Braveheart* film appeared to represent all of these attributes.'

Braveheart affected many peoples' sense of identity. Those who watched *Braveheart* in Scotland and around the world identified with a value system they liked. The film portrayed a sense of community, a sense of the value of the individual, the importance of family, of love. It questioned authority and privilege. The blue paint on the faces of Wallace and his followers (much berated by historians and critics alike) emphasised the difference between the nobles, who believed the people of Scotland were there to give them their position, and Wallace's gang, who believed their positions were created to give their people freedom.

Seoras Wallace of The Wallace Clan Trust supplied the chant 'MacAulish, MacAulish' shouted after Wallace slays the sheriff in revenge for the killing of Murron. *MacAulish* is Scottish Gaelic for 'son of Wallace'. The meaning of this phrase is one of the most frequently asked questions to the MacBraveHeart website.

Disrespect for the elite and a willingness to indulge in subversive activities characterised *Braveheart*'s Wallace. Instead of listening just to the nobles, the audience hears the conversation of the common man and his vision of what the battle means for him.

There was little sense of division portrayed between leader and follower in Wallace's army. Both were shown as fighting for a common cause and not for the acquisition of 'Lands and Titles'. This civic nationalism struck a chord round the world. Ironically,

Your site is exactly what the internet should be all about! I'm a huge 'Braveheart' fan. A few years back, I had to take custody of my two children, start a new business and deal with the murder trial of the kidnappers and killers of my friend's daughter. (All at the same time). Fortunately, believe it or not, I chose to watch Braveheart again and again for inspiration and hope during this very difficult period. Since I'm of Scottish heritage, I was learning just how brave they were through their struggles in an insanely cruel situation. Of course the film may not be accurate in every little detail, but it's the general historical story of William Wallace which gave me courage to keep the 'oars in the water'. Anyhow, my kids are doing great, my business is booming and my friend is moving on with her life slowly but steadily. I know a three hour movie can't fix things by itself, but it sure can get you thinking straight again. We all have to face our own battles head on and not run from them! And that's the real moral of the story of William Wallace.
Mike Burgess

Wallace's struggle in *Braveheart* to obtain representation for the people's wishes are set in a time when democracy as a concept did not exist.

> Just happened to find your website. I have the Braveheart DVD and soundtrack CD, and I, too, have seen this movie many, many times and still listen to the soundtrack. Great, great story, acting, attention to detail, filming, music . . . one of the greatest movies of all time. Although the Scots are rightly proud of this giant of a man, his story knows no culture, no national boundaries. I am a US citizen of Cuban and Spanish origin, and I too, along with all your other visitors, am impressed beyond measure with the courage of this Scot. (The only historical parallel that comes to mind – at least from my reference point – is Spain's El Cid.) I had never heard of WIlliam Wallace prior to Mel Gibson's movie. Now I can never forget him.
>
> Cesareo L. Fernandez

These *Braveheart* images of Scotland, the rags and the dirt, symbolised an oppressed country. Even the opening sweep of mountain and glen were not glimpsed in the breathtaking beauty of a summer's day. This imagery was not the intention in the original script. Here the Scottish nobles dressed in fine clothes like those of their English counterparts. But this imagery worked, despite all the criticisms, and it worked for one simple reason. People identified with the underlying concept that a man's worth is not measured by what he owns but by what he does.

Braveheart challenged many assumptions about Scotland and the Scots. It challenged the notion that Scotland could not go it alone. It reminded Scotland that beliefs were worth having. It showed Scotland that we are Scots before we are anything else; that the Scottish nation has much to be proud of in its history. It offered an image of a man who would not give up despite the pressures, the betrayals, the false Gods. And perhaps most strangely for many Scots, it rubbished the macho myth that a man can't say the words, 'I love you' and still be a man.

There are said to be ninety million people of Scots ancestry scattered about the world, eighteen times the current population of Scotland. There are also, according to our records, many people who, having seen *Braveheart*, would like to be Scottish. Certainly, for many Americans of Scots descent, *Braveheart* served as a wake up call. Most American children are required to research their family history as part of their school studies. With such a diverse racial group, this is one way of both demonstrating and celebrating the cultural richness of the American people. For many, the time and place of their forebears was suddenly displayed on the big screen in a format they could relate to. The reality of Scotland's past and the significance of Scotland's fight for survival left an indelible mark on many Americans who watched *Braveheart*. More than any other nation, Americans live in a society where people are measured by money. *Braveheart* was the antithesis of this, the story of a man who could not be bought no matter the circumstances. It was both a shock and a revelation.

> My grandparents and mother were born in Scotland. I grew up listening to the wonderful Scottish language and didn't realise how much I missed hearing it. Mel Gibson played the role of William Wallace so well that I believed he was William Wallace.
>
> Jim Morrison

For better or for worse, *Braveheart* has captured hearts for Scotland all around the world and continues to do so. As Paul Pender suggested in an article in the *Sunday Herald*, 'We have all been abroad on holiday and experienced that magical moment when previously hostile foreigners warm to us, as they realise a profound truth about the Scots – namely, that we are not the English. Their attitude is immediately transformed.'

Now such exchanges take on a William Wallace flavour.
'English?'
'No, Scottish.'
'Ah, *Braveheart*!' And a warm handshake.

Chapter Seven

The Movie
An Analysis

Randall Wallace explained how finding a 1722 copy of *Blind Harry's Wallace* in deep storage at the Library of Los Angeles made his hands shake. In it he found scenes that made Wallace come alive for him. Scenes which he later incorporated into *Braveheart*.

The emotional impact of the movie on both Scotland and its worldwide audience in 1995 reflected the emotional impact Blind Harry's telling of the Wallace story made on the people of Scotland in its own time.

Randall's reinterpretation of *Blind Harry's Wallace* as the movie *Braveheart* exploded on the scene at a time when Scotland was reassessing its future in a union with England. For many Scots, the movie posed questions not from the past, but of their present. In that respect it met Robert McKee's criteria for making an historical film. Randall, using *Blind Harry's Wallace* as inspiration and his skills as a dramatist [26] 'use[d] the past as a clear glass through which you show us the present.'

Using quotes from the original script, the following chapter attempts to interpret the movie in terms of its links with *Blind Harry's Wallace*, its political impact, particularly in Scotland, together with its historical accuracies and inaccuracies.

Act I

Wallace Raises his Head

Robert the Bruce begins the story of William Wallace. His voice sets the time and place of the *Braveheart* story with the opening narration. The image is stark, a country in turmoil.

I shall tell you of William Wallace. Historians from England will say I am a liar, but history is written by those who have hanged heroes.

The King of Scotland had died without a son, and the King of England, a cruel pagan known as Edward the Longshanks, claimed the throne of Scotland for himself. Scotland's nobles fought him, and fought each other over the crown. So Longshanks invited them to talks of truce, no weapons, one page only.

Among the farmers of that shire was Malcolm Wallace, a commoner with his own lands. He had two sons: John and William.

Scotland and England are at peace when Scotland's King Alexander III dies in a fall from a cliff at Kinghorn in March 1286 leaving Scotland without an heir to the throne. Edward I of England, apparently a trusted friend and neighbour, is asked to help decide the succession, there being thirteen claimants to the crown, with the Balliol and Bruce claims the strongest. Edward turns quickly from friend to foe, wishing Scotland for himself. The Scottish nobles, most of whom are of Norman descent and have lands in both Scotland and England, are divided amongst themselves as to who should have the crown.

The 'talks' spoken of in the opening narration refers to *Blind Harry*'s Bloody Barns of Ayr, where nobles were treacherously hung and slain

Went to the bloody barns, dreading not wrong.
A baulk was knit with cruel ropes and keen:
Oh! Such a slaughter house was never seen.

Edward I was a Christian king and not pagan, although he was a [27]'Plantagenet, a sept of the Angerins who had a dire reputation for evil'. Wallace's father was a minor noble, and considerably further down the social scale than Robert the Bruce.

The Irish and Scottish extras were very unhappy at the idea of the Irish fighting the Scots at the battle of Falkirk. They protested that the two countries had never been at war with one another. The script was changed because of this and they met in the centre of the battle as friends.

In the opening sentences of the narration, the impact of this re-telling of the Wallace story is foreseen. Wallace's story has always been an historic sword in the flesh, causing great controversy.

The device of using the survivor to tell a tale is a powerful one and has been used in a number of films, for example Roberto Benigni's 1997 film *Life is Beautiful* where the son tells the story of his dead father. This works particularly well if the survivor

---

I feel a need to tell you about my own Braveheart experiences.

First of all, I first saw Braveheart on opening day here in the States, mainly because I had heard, wrongly, that Mel Gibson exposed all. It was such a powerful movie that I remember leaving the theater believing that this was the best movie ever made. Then I read the review in Time Magazine, calling this movie unnecessary and inferior to 'Rob Roy', and began a personal vendeta to make everyone I knew see the movie.

Including the re-release, I saw Braveheart seven times in the theater.

In March, I received a wonderful birthday present. It was Oscar week, and Braveheart swept away the competition. It was a wonderful night.

In May, it came to the local pay-per-view channel, and I "borrowed" it off the airwaves to show to my European History teacher. She loved it. The day that the video came out, I skipped the first half of the school day, and bought not only the widescreen and re-formatted versions, but a TV-VCR for my room so that I could watch it any time I wanted.

Now that I'm a Freshman at the University of Illinois, I am continuing my crusade. Tonight I am re-directing a lost soul. I'm still not bored of the movie. It has every element that a 'movie' needs: it is gorgeous (a credit to the director for the vision, and the editing staff for realizing it), a beautiful love story, spectacular fight scenes, believable characters, raw emotions, comedy, and the ability to make you forget that it is three hours long. But, what a worthwhile three hours it is.

Patti Coil

owes his survival or success to the dead hero. In *Braveheart*, the character that grows the most is Robert the Bruce. His transformation from procrastinator to leading the fight for Scotland's freedom is a result of the example set by Wallace.

As the tale unfolds we see William's father and friends planning to fight back after the outrage of the Barns of Ayr. Young William wakens from a nightmare and overhears their plans.

> *Every nobleman who had the will to fight was at that meeting. We cannot beat an army. Not with the fifty farmers we can raise.*

> *We do not have to beat them – just fight them.*

His father will not let the young William go with them, despite his son's protestations that he can fight. Instead his father stresses the importance of brain over brawn.

> *I know you can fight. But it is our wits that make us men.*

This is the first time we see a sword and Wallace together. Similar sentiments are repeated in a later scene with his Uncle Argyle, where Argyle insists the young Wallace must learn to use his brain before being taught to use a sword. Already the sword has become symbolically linked with the protection of Scotland.

As William and Hamish play in sunshine, pretending to throw stones at an English patrol, William sets the scene for their future together, their play at the same time mimicking the fatal skirmish taking place at Loudon Hill. Unknowingly the young Wallace foretells the doom that is to befall his father.

> *It's up to us, Hamish.*

The smashing of the sheep skulls because of Wallace's already keen eye and accurate aim, lightens the scene as the two young boys play at fighting, unaware of the horror that awaits. Hamish is an invented character in the *Braveheart* story, although other characters in the movie can be directly linked to the characters in *Blind Harry* who form Wallace's gang.

The scene at his father's graveside has the priest speaking in

Latin, as everyone in Wallace's time was Roman Catholic. By the time of Hamilton of Gilbertfield's 1722 translation of *Blind Harry*, the Virgin Mary was transformed into Dame Fortune and St Andrew into King Fergus when they appear before Wallace at Monkton Kirk.

> It is difficult to claim that one has a favourite film with so many master-pieces out there, but for me personally I have to say Braveheart has to be it. I have the video here at home and when I get down or lose my courage in life I put on my favourite film and every time I cry, actually weep like a baby. This movie touches a special something with me. Maybe it is because I come from Scottish origins but more than that, it is the message that the most important lesson in life is to never compromise who you are and what you believe. William Wallace I pray will never be forgotten in history. He lived many years ago but to me he is still alive right here in my heart . . . my brave heart.
> Linda Calvert Valliant

In Scotland at this time, a number of languages would have been spoken, including English, Scots, Gaelic, Latin and French. Robert the Bruce's mother was a Gael and the use of Gaelic was more widespread throughout Scotland than is now the case.

Wallace was probably in his early twenties when his father was killed at Loudon Hill. However the gift of a thistle from one young child to another is a profoundly significant scene in the movie and has deeply moved people all over the world. As well as showing childlike compassion, the thistle itself represents Scotland. Thus, after his father is killed defending Scotland, the burden of his country's future is handed on to the young Wallace. As the story progresses we will come to see Murron and Scotland as one and the same.

The Uncle Argyle who arrives to collect William is a composite of the two uncles who were traditionally involved in his upbringing. One of these lived in Dundee and the other at Dunipace. It is the Dunipace uncle, a parish priest, who is said to have taught the young Wallace the following words, which our hero never forgot,

[28] *Freedom is best, I tell thee true, of all things to be one. Then never live within the bond of slavery my son.*

Later, young William dreams of his dead father whose advice

encompasses two of the three main themes of the movie: freedom and courage (love is the third).

Your heart is free. Have the courage to follow it.

Dream sequences play a significant part in Blind Harry's story of Wallace and the device is used well in *Braveheart* to signify high emotion and the connection between the dead and the living.

His uncle speaks of outlawed tunes on outlawed pipes which is a reference to a much later period in Scottish history when, after the Jacobite rebellion of 1745 tartan and the pipes were banned under the Act of Proscription on pain of transportation. Although many were quick to condemn tartan being used in *Braveheart* as a Hollywood misconception, countless past representations of Wallace, Bruce and the Wars of Independence have shown the wearing of tartan.

It was suggested by some that Randall Wallace should have used Nigel Tranter's 1975 novel *The Wallace* as a source. They seemed oblivious to the fact that Tranter also used *Blind Harry* as his main source. (It is by far the most extensive source for Wallace), [29] Nigel Tranter also had Wallace wearing a plaid *Braveheart*-style.

As Argyle talks to the boy, the words he uses reinforce the idea that Wallace will one day become an educated man, then a brilliant military strategist.

First learn to use this [*the head*]
Then I'll teach you to use this [*the sword*]

This is the second time young Wallace gets close to a sword, and this time he is allowed to handle it.

Mel Gibson asked Andrew Weir (young Hamish) if he knew anyone who might play the part of William as a young boy. Andrew proposed his friend James Robinson, who had never acted before. James Robinson did not want to continue acting after the movie, but decided later to pursue it as a career.

In the original screenplay, Randall has the Scottish nobles dressed in all their finery. In the movie, Scotland's nobles and people are dressed plainly or in rags, emphasising the state of oppression that grips the country. This aspect of the design also supports the theme of the worth of the common man, which surfaces again and again in the movie. A man's worth is not in his finery or noble birth, but in his heart.

By the time in history when Braveheart opens, Edward I had already garrisoned all the castles in Scotland and taken the law books south.

By way of contrast the next scene shows the royal finery of the English court where Edward's son is being married to the daughter of the French king. In terms of historical accuracy, Isabella would have been a baby at this time, and in no position to get married. The ceremony really encapsulates the way in which royal families marry amongst themselves not for love but to maintain their dynasties.

No words are spoken. We see characters in action; a nod of the head, a raised eyebrow, a puzzled look from Isabella, a steely stare from Longshanks, a disguised smile from the son's lover. Through these actions much is established about these characters, their thoughts, hopes and fears.

Edward II's lover was actually a young French knight, Piers Gaveston. In the whole span of the Middle Ages, only three English kings were deposed by violence, one of whom was Edward II. All three had a common failing, which largely contributed to their fate. They all had a taste for incompetent favourites who were loathed and despised by the nobles and people alike. But Edward's choice of favourite was the worst of all. His infatuation with Gaveston brought him both unpopularity and rebellion. [30] During the last years of his life Edward I banished Gaveston from court, but he was re-instated by Edward II after his father's death.

Princess Isabella proved to be a formidable opponent to her husband, making sure in the end he did not rule the kingdom for his allotted span. She had him tortured to death in 1327.

> *Scotland. My land. The French will grovel to anyone with strength, but how will they believe our strength when we cannot rule the whole of our own island?*

In terms of the Scottish consciousness, those words put into the mouth of an English monarch of seven centuries ago were indicative of present day circumstances in 1995. Just three years before the movie opened, the Conservative Party had been re-elected to govern the United Kingdom despite securing only 25% of the votes in

Scotland. A democratic deficit existed in Scotland for the entire period of Conservative power at Westminster, some eighteen years. For most of this period, the Conservative Prime Minister, Margaret Thatcher had been seen by many north of the border as the new Hammer of the Scots. In 1989, John McGrath's big theme play, *Border Warfare*, staged at the Tramway in Glasgow, depicted Mrs Thatcher as a latter day Boudicca coming north to hammer the Scots.

> My name is Jasna Stipanovic Durdevic. I am from Croatia.
> I have seen the movie 20 times and I am sure that I'll see it again.
> What a man, what a hero!!!
> And what to say about the scene – the gift of Thistle? The most tender scene in all history of movies.
> I cried for days because of this movie.
> And I can't get enough of it.

Braveheart's Edward tells us that nobles are the key to Scotland. Give them land in Scotland and they will do what they are told. The land issue is of fundamental importance in the Scotland of today, its outdated feudal laws having recently been revised by Scotland's new parliament.

With the increase in interest in Scottish history, many more Scots now know the story that the nobles of Scotland sold out in 1707 when they signed away the Scottish Parliament for English gold. Many believe Scotland is still being sold out by those who would like to keep rural Scotland empty of anything that can't be shot, and who would like control over Scotland's future to rest solely at Westminster.

The trouble with Scotland is that it's full of Scots.

Edward's line in *Braveheart* could be a quote from Prime Minister Margaret Thatcher's memoirs of the years in which she became almost universally hated north of the border. Plenty of political echoes there for a Scottish audience in 1995.

As Robert the Bruce continues with his story, he makes reference to a meeting of 'the council of Scottish nobles' in Edinburgh.

The first meeting of a parliament in Scotland was the Colloquium of 1235 at Kirkliston, in the reign of Alexander ii. The 'community of the realm of Scotland' is a concept that existed at the time of the 1320 Declaration of Arbroath, which sets down the unique position whereby sovereignty in Scotland lies with the people.

> [31] Yet if he should give up what he [King Robert] has begun, and agree to make us or our kingdom subject to the King of England or the English, we should exert ourselves at once to drive him out as our enemy and a subverter of his own rights and ours, and make some other man who was well able to defend us our King; for, as long as but a hundred of us remain alive, never will we on any conditions be brought under English rule. It is in truth not for glory, nor riches, nor honours that we are fighting, but for freedom – for that alone, which no honest man gives up but with life itself.

The Declaration of Arbroath is generally regarded as providing the blueprint of the 1776 American Declaration of Independence in which over half the signers were of recent Scots descent. The only clergyman to sign was the Rev. John Witherspoon, revered philosopher and academic who left St Andrews, Scotland to become Princeton University's first great president.

> *I was born and raised in a small town in the Smoky Mountains. of Tennessee, descended from the McCarters and the Carrolls and the Cotters. When I first saw Braveheart there was an immediate vibration in my own heart. It seemed as though I was watching my own life in another time. We own the video and it is watched with the same emotion each time and the same heartsong vibrates inside me at each viewing. If I close my eyes I can smell the heather and feel the mists on my face. Long live Sir William, the Braveheart.*

In James S. Adam's 1993 translation of the Declaration of Arbroath he states

> 'Almost alone among the nations of Feudal Europe where the accepted concept was that authority flowed downward from the crown, Scotland stated clearly and firmly that the rights flow upward, from the people.

This is reflected in the American Declaration of Independence.

[32] We hold these truths to be self-evident, that all men are created equal, that they are endowed by their Creator with certain inalienable Rights, that among these are Life, Liberty and the pursuit of Happiness. — That to secure these rights, Governments are instituted among Men, deriving their just powers from the consent of the governed, — That whenever any Form of Government becomes destructive of these ends, it is the Right of the People to alter or to abolish it, and to institute new Government, laying its foundation on such principles and organising its powers in such form, as to them shall seem most likely to effect their Safety and Happiness.

The Bruce is shifty in the council scene, displaying discomfort as he imparts to the nobles his father's wishes to play both hands.

My father believes that we must lull Longshanks into our confidence by neither supporting his decree nor opposing it.

The Bruces held land in Scotland, England and France; Robert the Bruce's father spent more time in England than in Scotland and is buried in England. Robert the Bruce spent a lot of his later life in Carrick in Scotland, although he spent time in the English court and was favoured by Edward I. This dual loyalty must have caused him great problems in deciding which way to turn politically. The suggestion that the Bruce's father was a leper is unfounded. It is more likely to have been Bruce himself who had leprosy. 1996 reconstructions, based on the skull of the Bruce from Dunfermline Abbey, suggest that he may have suffered from leprosy or a skin condition like psoriasis.

I speak for all the Bruces and for Scotland.

Unlike Wallace, Bruce sees ruling Scotland as his right.

Leaving the brooding corridors of power, we are plunged into a commoner's wedding, where camaraderie and love are the emotions in play. Wallace and Hamish meet again in a scene set to lighten the mood, while revealing the characters of both men. Hamish tries to pick a fight, Wallace refuses with humour, Hamish persists, and so Wallace beats Hamish at his own game. Like David and Goliath, like Asterix and Obelix, Wallace uses brain instead of brawn. He has learned well on his travels. He has also learned to use kindness and humour when dealing with women. He is a man of peace not easily driven to war. For the third time we are reminded,

A test of a soldier is not in his arm . . . it's here. [*head*]

We have not seen Wallace since he was a boy. What sort of man has he become? From his actions we see a man of humour and inner strength, a thinker, someone who does not forget his friends nor the place he grew up. He has travelled widely and now returned home. The community welcomes him back. They too have not forgotten. For a few minutes we believe that it is possible to live and love even in this occupied Scotland.

As Wallace joins in the game with Hamish, we are reminded of his aim and judgement. The setup in the earlier scene with his boyhood friend is now paid off as Hamish is felled by Wallace's pebble,

I should have remembered the rocks.

Cinema audiences understand the concept of setup and payoff and there are a number of these in *Braveheart*, usually at moments when the audience members need to laugh or have their spirits raised after a difficult and dark scene.

Just as we relax into the wedding scene and Wallace's reunion with Murron we are brutally reminded that, for all the gaiety of the day, Scotland is in a state of occupation, with a sherriff appointed to each town by the English. Although *prima nocte* was possibly a custom in Europe at this time, it was introduced here to Scotland for dramatic purposes. *Prima nocte* allowed the feudal overlord of an area to have sex with a woman on the night of her wedding, if he so wished. The essence of the feudal system, which underpinned Edward's attempted annexation of Scotland, is captured in the line:

It is my noble right.

Wallace does not fight at this point. He merely observes what Scotland has become.

Dark shifts to light. Wallace comes in search of Murron. They had great difficulty shooting this scene because of the weather and Mel decided just to go for it and brave the rain. The images of Scotland in rain and light brought emotional responses from people

who had left Scotland in their youth.
Braveheart would not have seemed so Scottish
had it not been for the distinctive light and
changeable weather in the early scenes.

> *It's good Scottish weather, madam. The*
> *rain is falling straight down . . . well,*
> *slightly to the side like.*

Scottish audiences knew what he was
talking about.

Wallace's romance with Murron features
large in Blind Harry's tale. He takes forty pages
to describe the length, breadth and depth of
Wallace's love for Marion. Wallace's sweet-
heart by tradition was Marion Braidfute of
Lamington. Her name was changed to Murron
for the movie because of concerns that there might be confusion
for a world audience with Robin Hood's Maid Marion.

At the 2000 *Braveheart* convention Marilyn Bannen was presented with a painting in memory of her late husband Ian Bannen. The painting 'I Belong Here' by Andrew Hillhouse was commissioned by the MacBraveHeart website and inspired by the scene from the movie where Wallace and Murron sit together on a mountain surveying the beauty of Scotland.

However there are claims in Scotland that Robin Hood is based
on the Wallace story, and the similarities are certainly very striking.
Wallace has his Marion; he has trouble with a Sheriff; he moves
around in disguise and hides out in woods; he fights for an absent
king; he is a bowman and is known to dress in green; he is loved
by the poor and feared by the rich. It all sounds very familiar.

In his courtship Wallace further convinces us of his intelligence
and his humour. He speaks to Murron in French and talks of Rome.

We know that Wallace travelled on the continent after defeat
at the Battle of Falkirk and a safe passage permit from the King of
France was found in his possession when he was captured. This
permit allowed him to travel to Rome. Wallace would have spoken
a number of languages. Many people would have been able to do
this in the Scotland of his time, where Gaels, Normans and Scots
existed side by side, and Latin was the language of the church.
Despite his travels, Wallace states his loyalty to his country simply
and powerfully,

> *But I belong here.*

As he leaves her at her home, Wallace's loyalty is further confirmed by his return of the thistle which Murron gave him as a boy and which he has kept with him (like a memory of Scotland) on his travels. Now Murron and Scotland are one; one in Wallace's love and his loyalty.

> *William Wallace was and IS a true hero from Scotland, but more important he is the symbol of honour, all over the world, an honour that nowadays sadly is forgotten. There are only a few men left in this world who can measure his courage. I myself come from a land were honour is priceless, and (but) feel Scottish when watching the movie. Thank you Mel for awakening one of the bravest hearts in the world history!*
>
> Ercan Ali Kosar (Turkish Dane)

Wallace is mending his roof (i.e. getting ready for marriage) when Campbell and MacClannough ride up. Campbell tries to encourage Wallace to join them at a meeting by reminding him of his father.

Your father was a fighter and a patriot.

Wallace's rebuff is plain, he knows who his father was, but he has come home to raise crops and a family. He wants to live in peace. However, this does not persuade Murron's father to let him court his daughter, and their 'no the noo' exchange is authentically Scottish. Interestingly Murron's father refers to Scotland's situation as 'the troubles', which is the term used to refer to the more recent problems of Northern Ireland. For a second time Wallace refuses to be drawn into the fighting.

We see Murron and Wallace in the grove together. The grove is symbolic in Celtic mythology and Christianity. As they talk Wallace manages to twist the conversation so that Murron in fact proposes to him. And hence the line that caused apoplexy in some quarters. A line no Scotsman, it was insisted, would ever say.

I love you. Always have. I want to marry you.

Wallace and Murron meet in the woods, beside a Celtic cross to exchange vows and handfasting-type cloths. The thistle-embroidered cloth that Murron gives Wallace is symbolic of both herself and Scotland. From now on the pressed thistle is replaced by the embroidered one. (second gift of a thistle)

> I've got a 1997 Jeep that I drive around in with the 'Waleis' name on the license plate, and a portrait of the 'Braveheart' Wallace on the tyre cover. It's gotten quite a response (not so good from the wife as she's embarrassed to drive it) from people yelling out 'Freeeeeedom', to an older Scottish couple who drove by waving with their own license plate . . . 'HILNDER'
> Great movie, great hero, great country . . . Scotland!
> M.Koz (East Dundee, Ill, USA)

I will love you my whole life; you and no other.

Wallace's declaration of love is as much to Scotland as to Murron. Both are to be tested beyond endurance.

For Randall Wallace those words are the most significant in the movie. As Randall says, not everyone will be true to their heart as William Wallace was to his, but that's the point of the movie, that Wallace was true to his heart.

From love and honour and loyalty we are plunged into the rape scene. The rape of Scotland by occupying forces becomes personal with the rape of Murron.

For Edward I the conquest of Scotland was very much a personal project. His representatives held all positions of authority in the country, while English soldiers garrisoned the Scottish castles. As Edward was about to leave for France he spoke with Surrey . . . Discussing tactics, he had every reason to believe what he was recommending would be the final solution for Scotland. Edward is recorded as ending the exchange with Surrey,

[33] *He does good business who rids himself of a turd.*

Murron is singled out for attack by the occupying soldiers simply to pass the time. This call to act can't be refused by Wallace. He fights to save his Murron.

As he helps her escape they arrange to meet at the symbolic grove. Wallace watches to make sure Murron is away safely (he thinks)

before he resumes the fight then makes his exit in disguise, a moment
of light relief amid the gathering darkness.

> *My name is Ernesto Baselga I am from Spain. I was a student at Preston
> University in England when Braveheart was on in Cinemas for the first
> time.*
> *The three hours of the movie flew away for me. God, I can't explain to you
> with words what I felt while I watched him love, fight and die with that
> passion and true sense of honour.*
> *Just try in my real life to look a little bit like him. My heart is not Scottish
> but is free.*

Reaching the grove Wallace waits for Murron but she will never
appear. The inciting incident is upon us; the incident that will drive
the protagonist into action until a resolution is found. The scene
that follows is the most traumatic in the movie, almost identical in
the choreography to Blind Harry's version.

> [34] *Where fled thy guardian angel in that hour,*
> *And left his charge to the fell tyrant's power?*
> *Shall his fierce steel be reddened by thy gore,*
> *And streaming blood distain thy beauties o'er?*
> *But now, awaken'd with the dreadful sound,*
> *The trembling matron threw her eyes around.*
> *In vain alas were all the tears she shed,*
> *When fierce he waves the faulchion o'er her head;*
> *All ties of honour by the rogue abjur'd,*
> *Relentless deep he plung'd the ruthless sword;*
> *Swift o'er her limbs does creeping coldness rise,*
> *And death's pale hand seal'd up her fainting eyes.*

As Murron searches the hillside for Wallace to save her we are
horrified by the thought of what is about to happen. As Murron's eyes
flicker shut, the sheriff drops her wedding cloth covered in blood
to the ground. The bond between Murron and Wallace has been
severed by death.

In *Blind Harry*, Marion dies at the hand of the Sheriff of Lanark
because Wallace runs through her house to make his escape. Wallace,

already an outlaw at this point, was not living openly with Marion in the house but had come to visit and was spotted at church.

In the movie, before the Sheriff kills Murron he talks of the application of English law in Scotland. As Edward moved to annex Scotland he was at great pains to work through the laws of the country removing any that conflicted with those in England.

And so ends the first act. Our hero, by the death of his love is driven to action.

Sir,

I am a boy from India. I don't entertain thoughts on people of other countries. We have enough heroes of our own here. There are many people projected as heroes in the papers and books – Washington, Churchill, Caesar, Napoleon, and many others, but we feel that they are not so great, and we always find a similar leader in India.

But then I saw Braveheart. I intended to see it just to spend my afternoon. While seeing it, and after seeing it, I just could not control myself. I was crying. I was feeling very sad. I felt that I'd lost somebody dear. I felt pain in my heart. I could not think of anything else than a man called 'William Wallace'.

I think I identify him as an Indian national hero. He may be a Scot. He may have been anyone. But I think we can relate to him. He seems to me 'a real hero'.

The way he rallies the Scots at Stirling, the way he goes about his job, the way he overcomes his fear, I think it must be emulated.

Ever since I saw that movie I have become William Wallace. I go about the neighbourhood shouting his dialogues. I take up an imaginary sword and rally the Indians against the English. I am now living a Wallace's life. I am trying to overcome fear of everything and become a brave heart.

Yours,

Venkata Prasad,

Tirupati, India.

Act II

Tests, Allies and Enemies

Going up Glen Nevis, it is possible to visit the location of the *Braveheart* Lanark village, if you know where to look, although the houses and fort are gone and the area restored.

The wooden fort has a place in the history of Scotland. Motte and bailey constructions were common before stone castles. [35] In Scotland there was no Norman Conquest in the English sense. We should speak rather of Norman penetration. Norman castles were not the ponderous stone keeps of popular imagination. The ordinary Norman castle was a thing not of stone and lime but of timbered earthwork – a moated mound crowned by a palisade enclosing a wooden tower.

The guerrilla tactics of Wallace began with the weapon hidden in his clothes as he approaches the English soldiers with his hands in the air. In *Blind Harry*, Wallace's successes are often achieved by trickery and ruse. Wallace was known to be nothing if not bold.

[36] Wallace's whole life demonstrated this boldness. Swift to act, brilliant in minor and then grand stratagems, fully prepared to adopt novel military formations, he had the nerve to take on the might of England's military power.

MacAulish. MacAulish. Wallace. Wallace.

After the Sheriff has been executed by Wallace, the rebel villages chant 'son of Wallace' in Gaelic, then 'Wallace, Wallace'. He has become leader by their choice and not his. This turning point completes the fusion of Scotland and Murron within Wallace. He has failed to protect Murron. She has been killed to get to him. If he cannot protect Murron, he can try at least to protect his country.

The death of Hazelrig, the Sheriff of Lanark at the hands of Wallace is documented and served as one of the charges at Wallace's trial. An eyewitness who feigned death, managed to survive and return to England to tell the tale.

[37] It has to be said that, incidentally from time to time, little morsels of evidence have turned up, serving curiously to confirm

the fundamentals of some of his (Blind Harry's) stories . . . The latter
part of the Hazelrig story being one. A Northumbrian knight, Sir
Thomas de Grey, had been taken prisoner in the Scots wars, and
was committed to the castle of Edinburgh. He wrote how in May
1297, his father was in garrison in Lanark, and that Wallace fell
upon the quarters at night, killed Hazelrig and set fire to the place.
His father had good reason to remember and tell about the affair,
for he had been wounded in it and left on the street for dead.

As Murron is buried, Wallace thinks back to his childhood
watching his father and brother being buried. He cannot forgive himself for being the cause of Murron's death. Her father sees fit to forgive him. The bond between the dead and the living is re-enforced.

After the darkness of death, the audience's tension must be
relieved. As Wallace ponders the bloody cloth (Scotland covered in
the blood of his wife), we are witness to the black humour of
Hamish's father, as they try to treat his wound and are left in no
doubt that this man has a will of iron.

That'll wake ye up in the morning, boy.

The MacGregors arrive from the next glen. (In Tranter's *The
Wallace*, a Stephen MacGregor plays a part in the Gargunnock Peel
incident.) The fusion of highland and lowland in *Braveheart* has
annoyed some critics, but in fact there was much greater integration
of the Gaelic culture throughout Scotland then than now. Also the significant omission of Andrew de Moray, who led the northern part of
the rebellion and was a commander at Stirling Bridge, is compen-
sated to a degree by the frequent inclusion of gaelic speech and
imagery, showing the large part played by the Highlands of Scotland
in the rising against Edward.

[38] Andrew de Moray raised his standard at Avoch in the Black
Isle, north of Inverness. By April 1297 he had raised the whole of
Moray against the English who maintained a strong presence in
the area, with large garrisons in the castles of Inverness, Urquhart,
Nairn, Forres, Elgin and Lochindorb.

*The Highlanders are coming down on their own.
Aye, in droves of hundreds and thousands.*

The *Braveheart* Wallace gang is being formed. Using guerrilla tactics they will work their way round Scotland taking castles back from the English then razing them to the ground. This was the method used by Wallace and later by Robert the Bruce. They could not garrison the captured castles themselves, so rather than let them be retaken by the English, they destroyed them or rendered them unusable.

Greetings from the frozen northeastern United States. There are movies and there are life changing cinema experiences, and Braveheart was one for me. It's a film I have a special feeling and reverence for, and great respect for William Wallace and the valiant struggle he waged so long ago. Mel Gibson, Randall Wallace and everyone involved did William proud. It's always heartening to see courage shown in it's true noble light and honour given its place above all else.

Alyn Syms

This scene seems to be based on the taking of Kinclaven castle in Tranter's *The Wallace*, where our hero kills Sir James Butler, puts on his surcoat, and gains entry to the castle, crying:

'I, William Wallace, call on all here to surrender! In the name of John, King of Scots!'

In *Braveheart* he continues:

Go back to England and tell them that Scotland's daughters and her sons are yours no more. Tell them Scotland is free.

It was impossible to witness the collective emotional response of a Scottish audience at this point in the movie, without feeling the enormous political resonance of the film in the Scotland of the 1990s.

The scene shifts back to England where we watch the reaction to Wallace's rebellion. By the spring of 1297, Edward believed he had secured Scotland. The previous year, he had massacred the inhabitants of Berwick, defeated the Scots in the battle of Dunbar, and sent 'Toom Tabard' (King John Balliol) to the Tower of London. The sack of Berwick was filmed for *Braveheart* but dropped from the final cut. Edward had already removed the Stone of Destiny and the Holy Rood of St Margaret, and was in the process of rewriting Scotland's history. Then Wallace raised his head.

Edward II argues with his father about Wallace, calling him a brigand, nothing more, a popular representation south of the border. The King is constantly angry with his son, showing distaste and even hatred at times. In his eyes his son is a weakling.

Throughout *Braveheart* the father/son relationship is explored; the Bruce and his father, Wallace and his father, Hamish and his father; Edward II and his father. We are shown sons born through love, having good relationships with their fathers, whereas those born in order to continue a dynasty have loveless relationships (Edward and his son) or difficult relationships (Bruce and his father). Dynasty is about holding onto or extending power, whatever the human cost.

As the rebellion develops in Scotland, there is a further pay off with a pebble, as the English commander corners a small group of Wallace's men against a cliff, only to have his question

Where's Wallace?

answered by a stone to his helmet. Wallace is proving to be as wily and clever as we were led to believe in earlier scenes.

Robert the Bruce comes to his father, full of news of the rebellion. His enthusiasm is brought to heel by his father, who reminds him of his position in the scheme of things. The Bruce is inspired by Wallace, by his passion and commitment. The son speaks to his father from the heart. His father replies in terms of money, land and titles.

> *You admire this man, this William Wallace. Uncompromising men are easy to admire. He has courage ... so has a dog. But it is exactly the ability to compromise that makes a man noble. And understand this: Edward Longshanks is the most ruthless king ever to sit on the throne of England. And none of us, and nothing of Scotland will remain, unless we are as ruthless. Give ear to the nobles. Knowing their minds is the key to the throne.*

When the Bruce fights it will be to win the throne. For Wallace the fight is about saving his country and its people. As for his father's description of the character of Longshanks, history has proved it to be true.

Back in England, we hear of the pursuit of Wallace through conservation between Princess Isabella and her maid. Wallace is a brigand, a thief. He must be destroyed and to flush him out they will desecrate his lover's grave. Despite the danger to himself, Wallace has rescued his lover's body and taken it to a secret place. The scene where Wallace rescues his wife's body was in both the original screenplay and Randall Wallace's novel but not filmed for the movie.

Isabella, who longs for love and can find none in her own marriage, or in the family she has joined, is captivated by these deeds of Wallace. Isabella's dreamy romantic view of Wallace is quickly contrasted with the reality. Wallace sits with his gang round a campfire, tearing meat from bones and discussing the tactics of war and other manly things.

Eventually Longshanks will send his whole Northern Army against us.

Heavy cavalry, armored horse; shake the very ground.

They'll ride right over us.

Uncle Argyle used to talk of it; how no army had ever stood up to a charge of heavy horse.

So what will we do?

Hit run hide, the Highland way.

Looking up into the trees, Wallace says:

We'll make spears. Hundreds of them. Long spears, twice as long as a man.

That long?

Aye.

Some men are longer than others.

Your mother been telling stories about me again. Eh?

The laughter is genuine, a relief from their real thoughts. They will abandon the small scale guerrilla tactics employed up to now. Wallace has decided it is time to meet Edward's army head on. Such a move requires more than just courage. It will demand a mind that is both brilliant and creative.

Wallace's men are right to fear the armoured horse. Although in the movie the number of horses used in filming was one hundred and fifty, the number is put at nearer [39] two thousand. The Scots army did not have anything like that number of horsemen, and these were under the command of James the Steward, and Malcolm, Earl of Lennox. Standing against a charge of such a large mounted force would have been suicidal for foot soldiers.

The hit-run-and-hide method had been used to deal with invading forces throughout Scottish history, where these forces greatly outnumbered the defenders: from the time of Calcagus leading the Picts against the Romans. The spears that Wallace suggests they use allow the formation of shiltrons, actually first used by Wallace's army at the later Battle of Falkirk and in 1314, to much greater effect, by Bruce at the Battle of Bannockburn.

The gang's discussions are interrupted by the arrival of Faudron and Stephen of Ireland. Both Faudron and Stephen are to be found in Blind Harry's epic poem where Faudron tries to betray Wallace and Wallace has to kill him.

From a hundred years before the time of Wallace, England had been trying to enforce its rule on Ireland. After Bannockburn, Robert the Bruce campaigned against the English in Ireland. Bruce's brother Edward became High King of Ireland in 1316, and almost captured Dublin the following year, fighting the English near where the *Braveheart* battle scenes were filmed.

Stephen of Ireland was a wonderful character who brought great passion and humour to the movie. His claim that

In order to find his equal, an Irishman is forced to talk to God.

is in direct contrast to the oft-voiced stereotypical view of the Irish as stupid.

My name is Gene Kutzler (not Scottish at all). I fell in love with Scotland on a trip my wife and I took about 10 years ago. The people where the friendliest I've ever met. Since that time I have learned to play the bag-pipes and started a small folk group singing Scottish songs. I think Braveheart showed the bravery and stamina of a small country just trying to be itself. With England trying to rule everyone and everything through-out history, Scotland and its people had to struggle long and hard to stay free as long as it did. I enjoy reading about Scottish history and would love to visit there again, and since getting interested in Scotland, I have found out my great grandmother's name is Elizabeth McCleary, so she must have been calling me to where she came from.

Stephen was also used to clearly identify the impossibility of their position. As Hamish suggests,

You're a madman.

Stephen replies,

I've come to the right place then.

The audience is horrified when they are led to believe that Stephen is trying to kill Wallace and very relieved when he turns out to be Wallace's guardian angel.

Sure didn't the almighty send me to watch your back? I didn't like him anyway. He wasn't right in the head.

And so the tables are turned. The mad man is in fact the wise man. The idea that a mad man is closer to God is not uncommon, for example some African cultures treat mad men with respect, believing a mad man capable of great wisdom. Charles Dickens in David Copperfield gave Mr Dick a similar place.

Wallace is respected, even loved by his men. They will follow him anywhere. They want to protect him. He listens to what they have to say. Their relationship is egalitarian. Contrast this with Edward who never takes advice.

Who is this who speaks to me as though I needed his advice?

Edward does not rule by love and loyalty, but by fear and intimidation.

Wallace's army at the real Battle of Stirling Bridge was predominately an army of commoners. There were very few nobles. Andrew de Moray had come down from the north and he and Wallace fought the battle as joint commanders. Andrew de Moray received a wound at the battle that was to prove fatal. The omission of de Moray from the movie was perhaps the greatest historical inaccuracy, for de Moray played such an important part in the freeing of Scotland. His banner is now ceremonially raised each year in the village of Avoch on the Black Isle.

It is fitting that the movie should feature the lot of the common man in the battle. Peter Mullan, playing the veteran tells us their view of the proceedings.

I didn't come here to fight so that they can own more lands. Then I have to work for them.

[40] Scotland, especially the Highlands, has provided a disproportionate number of soldiers per head of population in the UK. During the Crimean and First World Wars, large numbers of men were persuaded to enlist by the highland landowners who were their feudal superiors and thus held great power. While these men were away fighting for king and country, their families were driven out and their crofts burned down during the infamous Highland Clearances.

The *Braveheart* Battle of Stirling was a subject of criticism. There are many sources of reference[41] should you want to know all the details of the military tactics used by Wallace against 'The largest army in Christendom'.

The bridge does appear in the original screenplay by Randall Wallace, together with the battle method used by Wallace. Why these don't appear in the final movie is not clear. A complex mix of reasons seems to be the answer; cost, location and use of horses in a potentially dangerous situation.

We do know for sure that Wallace was tall. He would have to be to wield that sword, all 5ft 7ins of it as seen in the display at the National Wallace Monument, Stirling. In the original script no

mention is made of Wallace's height as he enters the crowds of soldiers. However Gibson pays homage to Wallace's height and the
stories about him through dialogue with the young soldier.

Sons of Scotland . . . I am William Wallace.

William Wallace is seven feet tall.

*Yes I've heard. He kills men by the hundreds and if he
were here he'd consume the English with fireballs from his
eyes and bolts of lightning from his arse. I am William
Wallace! And I see a whole army of my countrymen here
in defiance of tyranny. You have come to fight as free men
and free men you are. What will you do with that freedom? Will you fight?*

The reference to free men is borne out in evidence of the time,
as discussed in *Wallace* by Peter Reese.

[42] Across Scotland as a whole men tended to have more freedom
than the rest of Europe. This applied not only to the great provincial
lords or the proud rulers of Galloway and Argyle but to many in the
close knit burghs and on royal estates in Lothian and Strathclyde . . .
This significant proportion of free men were frequently self confident,
proud and robust individuals . . . As a result, a strong sense of indi-
viduality and love of freedom has grown up (in Scotland), a quality
accentuated by the country's geographical characteristics.

Free to choose or not, the veteran soldier is quick to point out the
strong possibility of annihilation with the odds ranged against them.

Fight against that? No, we will run and we will live.

And so to the speech that stirred a nation on the brink of self-
determination:

*Aye. Fight and you may die. Run and you'll live. At least
a while. And dying in your beds many years from now,
would you be willing to trade all the days from this day
to that, for one chance, just one chance to come back here
and tell our enemies that they may take our lives, but
they'll never take our freedom?*

As well as resonating with Scots, this speech provided *Total Film Magazine*'s Best Movie Dialogue of the Millennium.

They may take our lives, but they'll never take our freedom.

Both audience and cast reacted powerfully to this scene. As Randall states at the beginning of Chapter 1, Mel Gibson was the 20th century audience's William Wallace, every bit as much as *Blind Harry*'s *Wallace* served the audience of the 15th to the 18th centuries.

Braveheart presented a Wallace that rang true to audiences in Scotland and around the world. [43]A Wallace, wondrously brave and bold, of goodly mien and boundless liberality.

[44]*Blind Harry* (*Braveheart*) certainly succeeds in stirring our emotions and, whatever his reasons, its author leaves us in no doubt that, during his lifetime and beyond, Wallace represented (represents) an immensely powerful symbol for Scottish independence.

On the English side, as in the movie, the two leaders were in dispute as to how the battle should be conducted. Edward 1 had issued terms to be delivered and the English commanders would have no reason to think that the battle was anything but a foregone conclusion. After all they held all the cards. [45]Estimates run at 10,000 men for the Scots, mostly foot soldiers, and 50,000 for the English. The Scottish cavalry was vastly inferior to the English and under separate control of the nobles.

The painted faces of Wallace and his followers irritated some, yet woad was worn at the Battle of the Standard one hundred years prior to Stirling Bridge. Wallace has the Saltire painted on his face in *Blind Harry*, where the idea probably originated.

When Wallace rides out to pick a fight, he declares Scotland's terms and not his own, strengthening the concept that he fights not for himself but for Scotland and that Scotland is not owned by nobles but by its people.

He also accuses the English of 100 years of theft, rape and murder which is untrue, since there had been around a hundred years of peace between the two countries until Edward 1 brought it to an end.

The battle scenes though black and violent, contain much Scottish humour. Mornay's comment after the pick-a-fight scene

I'd say that was rather less cordial than he was used to.

being one instance.

Mooning and lifting of kilts shows the defiance of the Scots in what looks like a no-win situation. Stephen of Ireland is also used to lighten the tension after the first volley of arrows.

The Lord says He can get me out of this mess, but He's pretty sure you're fucked.

The priests blessing the army acknowledges Catholicism being the religion of the time. Wallace as a Catholic has become acceptable although Scotland's Catholic heritage has at times in the past been suppressed because of the Calvinist influence.

At the battle of Stirling Bridge, Wallace forced his army to wait until he chose the time for attack, holding his men until at least one third of the English army had crossed the bridge before sounding his horn. A similar waiting tactic was used in the film as the thundering horses approached. Campbell's prediction that the English cavalry would shake the very ground proves well founded.

After Wallace delivers his ultimatum, the English commander decides he wants Wallace's heart on a plate for his insolence. At this point Stewart, a soldier with the Scot's army, shouts,

You bastards.

This character was played by Mel Gibson's brother.

The determination and ferocity of the Scots attack must have come as a surprise to those in charge on the English side.

[46] For all English observers that day, whether they had made any attempt to understand the behaviour of the opposition, or not, the relish the Scots showed for fighting and their implacability must have been awesome.

Towards the end of the battle sequence Wallace kills Cheltham, the leader of the English army. *Blind Harry* also has Wallace killing the English leader, beheading him.

It is not known for certain that Wallace killed Cressingham, one of the leaders of the English army, although it is likely that both

Wallace and de Moray were in the thick of the battle. Cressingham was both feared and hated by the Scots, having indulged in nefarious activities during his reign of power in Scotland.

> [47] Cressingham was as highly unpopular with his own troops as he was with the Scots. He was despised by many of the nobles as a bastard and a vain self opinionated man who had misappropriated for his own use some of the dues designated towards the rebuilding of Berwick.

> [48] It is rumoured that Cressingham was skinned after the battle by Wallace or some of his followers in revenge for past misdeeds or perhaps in revenge for the mortal wound received by de Moray.

The battle ends with another chant of **Wallace, Wallace,** reminiscent of El Cid. Wallace is now Scotland and Scotland Wallace. The local scale of the uprising has turned national. All the constituent parts for an epic movie are now in place.

After the battle, Wallace is made Guardian of Scotland. (True, with Wallace probably knighted by Robert the Bruce in the Kirk o' the Forest in Selkirk.) As Hamish receives his medal from Wallace (Brendan Gleeson says his medal is his most treasured possession from *Braveheart*), Bruce seeks Craig to find out more of the man.

Does anyone know his politics?

No but his weight with the commoners can unbalance everything.

Robert the Bruce reveals by his question, the eternal dilemma: Does fighting for Scotland's independence make Wallace a fully paid up member of the Scottish National Party? Certainly *Braveheart* was used for SNP propaganda directly after the movie was released which seemed to many to smack of opportunism.

Craig's words did prove to be true in a modern sense. The *Braveheart* Wallace proved so popular with the 'commoner' that some people worried it might 'unbalance everything' in a time of great political change.

Onscreen arguments and fighting break out between the Balliol and Bruce factions. By this time in history, Balliol having already been made a puppet king by Edward I and been stripped of his power and put in the tower of London.

In the movie, the constant arguments between the opposing factions give Wallace the opportunity to lecture the nobles on their obsession with their own advancement to the detriment of Scotland. He tells them he will invade England. The nobles are flabbergasted and tell him it is impossible. Wallace asks:

Why? Why is it impossible? You're so concerned with squabbling for the scraps from Longshanks' table that you've missed your God given right to something better. There is a difference between us. You think the people of this country exist to give you position. I think your position exists to give those people freedom. And I go to make sure that they get it.

This speech closely reflected the political feelings of many people in Scotland leading up to the 1997 General Election and Referendum. The Conservative Party suggested devolution wasn't a good idea because Scotland was financially dependent on England. The Labour Party told Scots not to vote for independence, only for devolution, because we were financially dependent on Westminster and couldn't go it alone.

Outside Bruce and Wallace argue, Bruce putting forward the argument that the more you have the more you have to lose.

I respect what you said, but remember that these men have lands and castles. It's much to risk.

Wallace sees things differently.

And the common man that bleeds on the battlefield, does he risk less?

Bruce indicates what the real problem is for the nobles at least.

No, but from top to bottom this country has no sense of itself. Its nobles share allegiance with England.

It could be argued that Wallace created Scotland as a nation, uniting as he did all the different groups of people to fight at Stirling Bridge. Because of this, Wallace is often seen as the Founder of the Nation. When Robert the Bruce won the throne, he stopped the nobles having land in both countries. If they accepted their Scottish title and lands they were required to give up any held in England.

> I am Scottish of Scottish blood and I live in Scotland. I first saw Braveheart on its release here. There's no denying it's a powerful film. It reached something inside of me that was lost, or at least dormant. The fight for freedom in Scotland has long since become a political one, our fortunes have wavered, the highland clearances at the hands of the English in the late 18th and early 19th century, saw that any pockets of rebellion, any notions of freedom, were forever wiped out. My own ancestors avoided deportation only by coming south to the industrial centres in Glasgow and the like. However, just by spending time in Scotland's rugged and unforgiving landscape, you do achieve a sense of what Wallace fought for. Many of my countryfolk have not ventured from their cities into the Highlands of Scotland. We know too little of our own history and sometimes it seems as though all that Wallace fought for is lost. 'Even yet, from top to bottom this country has no sense of itself'. Perhaps we may get there, if we can just rediscover the spirit of Wallace. Thanks for this website it's really nice to see that Scotland has become a focus for such affection and admiration!! We have this marvellous movie to thank for that.
>
> John Beaton

Bruce tells Wallace:

I'm not a coward. I want what you want.

But what is he prepared to risk to get it? After Wallace's execution, Bruce did rise and take the crown, losing everything but his courage: family, land and titles, and being excommunicated from the church.

And all the time Wallace throws the questions at the Bruce. Why can't we do this? Why do we need the nobles? What does it mean to be noble? Through his direct questions, Wallace challenges deeply held beliefs of the day, almost convincing the Bruce that the impossible might be possible.

In both *Blind Harry* and *Braveheart*, Wallace sacks York, although in reality Wallace got only within sight of York. *Blind Harry* has Wallace besiege York and burn the gates.

> *Then unto York they march'd without delay,*
> *No sin they thought it there to burn and slay . . .*
> *Burn'd to the gates and suburbs of the town.*

York was indeed a staging post for many invasions of Scotland, from the late 11th century onwards.

Edward 1 himself spent huge amounts of time and money trying to subdue Scotland, becoming completely obsessed with it. Edward's remains lie in a crypt in Westminster Cathedral. He gave orders he was not to be buried. Instead the flesh should be boiled from his bones and the bones carried with the army until his son succeeded in subduing Scotland.

Although Edward professes to be concerned that Wallace would invade lower England in the movie and *Blind Harry* also has it that way, there was little chance of that. Instead Wallace spent his time raiding northern England.

Edward decides to send the Princess to offer Wallace a truce and buy him off. In *Blind Harry*, Edward sends his wife.

Dream scenes are a recurring feature in both *Blind Harry* and *Braveheart* and provide a link between the dead and the living – young Wallace with his father, Wallace with Murron; both provide Wallace with a continuing reminder of what he must do for Scotland.

So Wallace meets with Longshanks' Queen in *Blind Harry*, and Princess Isabella in *Braveheart*. Both of them rather liked Wallace.

> *Some said the queen did Wallace much admire,*
> *Who daily so much honour did acquire,*
> *And in her heart, by far did him prefer*
> *To most of men for his brave character;*

Reading *Blind Harry*'s version of events, the tent scene in *Braveheart* unfolds before our eyes.

> *And he tells her what has happened,*
> *How Edward made him prisoner at Ayr,*

Broke a strict truce and hang'd our barons there.
How Hasilrig kill'd his beloved wife,
And therefore would hate South'ron during life.
The silver tears (great pity to behold)
Came trickling down when he his tale had told.

Wallace tells the Princess of the Sack of Berwick and speaks to her in both French and Latin, confounding Hamilton who has called him a savage.

I never lie. But I am a savage. (homo indomitus –
unconquerable man)

The fact that Wallace speaks to the Princess on equal terms (as in *Blind Harry* with the Queen) is in direct contrast to the picture we are given of her relationship with both her husband and father-in-law.

When the Princess says,

I understand you have recently been given the rank of knight.

Wallace is angry, answering,

I have been given nothing. God makes men what they are.

She tempts Wallace with offers of gold, titles and land. Wallace rejects them all,

A lordship and titles, that I should become Judas?

This scene is reminiscent of Jesus' temptation in the desert and Randall is quoted as saying,

'I had already found a shape for my story (the William Wallace of *Braveheart* follows the pattern of Jesus of Nazareth as told in the Gospels) but finding *Blind Harry* gave me new material and insight, such as the incident with the Princess, though I changed her age and made her the wife of Edward II, while Harry made her the wife of Longshanks.'

As she travels back south the Princess gives away the gold that Wallace has scorned, just as the Queen does in *Blind Harry*.

I gave it to ease the suffering of the children of the war.

The fact that Wallace scorns the gold is in direct contrast to the behaviour of the nobles. Wallace's understanding of Longshanks' notion of peace is well founded as the Princess discovers on her return.

In his final words to the Princess, Wallace echoes the sentiments of the later Declaration of Arbroath.

You tell your king that William Wallace will not be ruled, and nor will any Scot while I live.

It is a challenge that Edward cannot resist. Wallace states he will await Edward's arrival in York, just as in *Blind Harry*, however the duplicity of Edward is revealed on the Princess's return with Wallace's message. Edward's plans are already in motion to reach Scotland ahead of Wallace and turn Scotland to ashes.

In fact Wallace and his army operated a scorched earth policy to try to defeat Edward. Knowing the size of the army that needed fed, they removed all possibility of finding food in front of the advancing English army, hoping to force an eventual withdrawal.

The Princess has warmed to Wallace on the first occasion she meets him. Now she helps him a second time, warning him of Edward's plans via her French maid. (Both the French Princess and her maid provide a metaphor for the French support of Scotland against England.)

On the way back to Scotland, news is brought of the imminent arrival of English ships and Irish troops. In Randall's original script the Scots only see the Irish troops once the battle lines are drawn. Crossbows also feature in the original script, with Wallace being warned about these by the Princess via her maid. Crossbows had already been outlawed by the Pope because of their accuracy and ferocity. In the movie, longbows were substituted for crossbows and long lines of spears replaced the Schiltrons.

In advance of Falkirk, Wallace tries to rally the nobles to no avail.

If you will not stand up with us now then I say you are cowards. And if you are Scotsmen, I am ashamed to call myself one.

The Bruce leaves the nobles and speaks to Wallace alone, urging restraint.

Now you've achieved more than anyone ever dreamed, but fighting these odds it looks like rage, not courage.

Wallace will not be turned. He pleads with the Bruce to help him defend Scotland against the invaders.

It's well beyond rage. Help me. In the name of Christ help yourselves. Now is our chance, now. If we join we can win. If we win, well then we'll have what none of us have ever had before: a country of our own.

Immediately after this personal confrontation between Wallace and Bruce, we see the Bruce's father urging him to do the opposite. Wallace has spoken to the Bruce with passion. Now his father talks coldly to him of dynasty and power, trying to convince him it is not for himself, but for his country that he must turn traitor. A noble need not stand by his word, when power is at stake.

I gave him my word.

I know it is hard. Being a leader is.

Most people were shocked to see Bruce on the wrong side at the Battle of Falkirk in *Braveheart*. However this was as portrayed in *Blind Harry*. Edward was at the battle. He had been injured the evening before by his horse and insisted on riding it in the battle although in great pain with a broken rib. The Scots army position was betrayed to Edward the night before the battle, thus forcing them to fight instead of continuing their retreat towards Stirling.

Edward begins by sending in the Irish instead of the archers.

Not the archers. My scouts tell me their archers are miles away and no threat to us. Arrows cost money. Use up the Irish. Their dead cost nothing.

The defection of the disposable Irish to the Scottish side gives the audience the impression that luck might be with the Scots after all. In the original screenplay, the Irish do charge the Scots.

However when it came to filming, there was said to be much dismay from the Irish and Scots about fighting one another, so the scene was changed to have the Irish switch sides, leading to one of the most popular scenes in the movie, especially for those of Irish descent.

Mornay and Lochlan lead their cavalry off the field and Edward tells his general,

I gave Mornay double his lands in Scotland and matching estates in England. Lochlan turned for much less.

Audiences were horrified when it was revealed that Mornay and Lochlan had betrayed Wallace for land and titles in England. In the usual Hollywood movie, the hero wins. In *Braveheart*, the first-time audience could not believe that Wallace might lose this battle. As the cavalry desert the field, led by a smirking Lochlan, the audience begins to realise the depth of the deceit. (Cavalry did ride off at Falkirk under the Red Comyn, leaving the Scots archers unprotected. They in turn could not protect the Schiltons from the Welsh bowmen. So the loss of the cavalry probably was decisive).

As Wallace tears the helmet from his opponent's head, both audience and Wallace together share the full power of the treachery against him. Earlier when Hamish said,

The Bruce is not coming, William,

Wallace had answered with conviction,

He'll come. Mornay and Lochlan have come. So will The Bruce.

Now the truth is revealed. The Bruce is here but on the opposite side. Bruce and Wallace stare into one another's eyes, before Wallace collapses back, exhausted by both his physical and spiritual wounds. In the Bruce's eyes, Wallace has seen what it means to be 'noble', how little Robert the Bruce will risk for Scotland. This is the dramatic low point for the Bruce.

This scene between Bruce and Wallace is the face-off between truth and lies; between the ordinary man willing to die for his country, and those who see war as a means to a more powerful end. Mel Gibson's portrayal of Wallace's pain at this moment brought great acclaim from audiences. Angus McFadyen's portrayal of the Bruce in his realisation of what he has done was equally moving.

In some historical sources the Bruce is said to have arrived late at the battle and then been responsible for saving Wallace. The scene as shot in *Braveheart* was not faithful to the original script either. In Randall's screenplay, Wallace first saves Hamish's father by putting him on a horse, then meets Bruce head on in battle as in *Blind Harry*. Shocked and horrified when he realises who the knight is, Wallace will not fight, although the Bruce urges him to. Stephen rides in and knocks down the Bruce and pulls Wallace onto the horse.

As Wallace is carried off, the Bruce picks up Murron's wedding cloth from the grass. Now the care of Scotland is in his hands. This was true as Wallace's political power ended at the Battle of Falkirk.

Bruce wanders through the horror that is the battlefield, as women search for the bodies of their husbands and children for their fathers. As Bruce sinks to his knees, Scotland dying around him, he realises the true result of his betrayal of Wallace.

The next two scenes contrast the father/son relationships of the Bruce and Hamish. Hamish's father is dying and Hamish cannot accept this and urges him tearfully to live. His father however is content to die.

> *I've lived long enough to live free; proud to see you become the man you are; I'm a happy man.*

The Bruce and his father meet in verbal combat, the son despising his father for what he, the son has become.

> *You saved your family, increased your land. In time you will have all the power in Scotland.*

> *Lands, titles, men, power, nothing.*

> *Nothing?*

Ian Bannen played the Bruce's father with force, passion and persuasion. His character symbolised all that was rotten in the Scottish hierarchy of the time. The rotting figure echoes 'Nothing?' in disbelief, as if he, the father has no conception of what his son means, valuing as he does only land, wealth and power, while his son is discussing his heart and his soul. Up to now the Bruce has echoed Scotland's nobles and their prevarication. From now on things will be different. The Bruce declares,

I will never be on the wrong side again.

Now a dream sequence is used to show the force of Wallace's revenge on those who betray Scotland. *Braveheart* is rich in texture, using different imagery to convey powerful emotions. In Faudron's Dream in *Blind Harry*, Wallace jumps through a high window to escape, as he does after killing Mornay. *Blind Harry* has again been used as a toolbox to give substance to the man.

Meanwhile Craig is worried that he might be next on Wallace's list after Mornay. Wallace, he believes is,

More of a liability than ever he was.

Craig and his fellow nobles do not know what to do with Wallace. He is not of their class, does not think or act like them, and he speaks up for Scotland against anyone, even them.

In this scene we see Robert the Bruce beginning to turn, adopting a different view from the other nobles; almost adopting a death wish to atone for his own involvement in the betrayal of the Scots at Falkirk. As the nobles talk of the possibility of Wallace taking his revenge on them, the Bruce says,

Maybe you, maybe me. It doesn't matter.

The blood that drips onto Craig's hands as he eats has a story source, though it refers to Bruce, rather than Craig. After a battle, in which Bruce fought on the wrong side, he sat down to dinner among his southern friends and allies, without washing his hands, on which there still remained spots of blood. The English Lords, observing this, whispered in mockery, 'Look at that Scotsman, who is eating his own blood'.

Shocked and disgusted at himself the Bruce vows to atone for this by doing all in his power to deliver Scotland from the foreign yoke.

After the body of Lochlan hits the table, we see Wallace running along a mountain path. This scene, with the picture of Wallace, the country for which he fights spread out below him, proved to be a powerful one for those watching.

If you slow down the scene in which Lochlan falls on the table, you can see he is definitely not a true Scot as he is wearing underpants!

The legend grows (and still does). *Braveheart's* Wallace is spoken of in hushed tones. Historically, Wallace had reverted to outlaw status and had gone overseas to plead Scotland's case with the King of France and the Pope.

[49] On 7 November 1300 the French king gave Wallace a letter of authority for presentation to his French officials in Rome. This asked them to assist Wallace in any appeal he might make to the papal court against actions taken by the English king over Scotland.

His legend grows. It will be worse than before.

Ironically it was by killing Wallace in the way he did, that Edward made Wallace a legend.

Wallace meets the Princess for the second time (stories often operate in threes, because people subconsciously like threes. So there's one meeting to go after this, in the cell).

Edward sends the Princess to trap Wallace. If she is killed, the King of France could become ally to the English rather than the Scots. The Auld Alliance between Scotland and France dates from Wallace's time.

The romance between the Princess and Wallace is a figment of the dramatist's imagination, although arguably essential to the dramatic structure of the epic movie.

In *Scottish Chiefs*, the hugely popular novelised version of the Wallace story of 1810 (so much so Napoleon banned it as dangerous), Jane Porter goes one further than Randall Wallace and gives Wallace a new wife whom he marries in his prison cell. She says in her introduction,

'Other private events have been interwoven with the public subjects of this volume, that the monotony of a continued series of warlike achievements might in some measure be lessened.'

The scene where Wallace burns the soldiers in the barn comes from *Blind Harry's* Barns of Ayr incident but it is out of time sequence here. This action was carried out in reprisal for the earlier hangings in the barn.

Although Wallace outwits Edward and his assassins at this time, his days are numbered.

[50] Wallace was captured on 3 August 1305. The man responsible was Sir John Menteith, a Scot who had made peace with Edward in 1304. Edward rewarded Menteith by granting him sheriffdom of Dumbarton and making him keeper of the castle.

It is suggested Wallace was on his way to meet with the Bruce in an effort to spark off the uprising again, when his position was betrayed at Robroyston in Glasgow, by one of his servants, Jack Short. Menteith delivered Wallace to Sir Aymer de Valence and Sir Robert de Clifford, who took him south to Carlisle Castle where he was imprisoned in 'Wallace's Tower'. After Carlisle, Wallace was handed over to Sir John Segrave, who took him south to London. The journey took seventeen days.

As Hamish warns Wallace not to go to the meeting with the Bruce despite the evidence of Murron's wedding cloth, Hamish tells Wallace:

I don't want to be a martyr.

Nor I. I want to live. I want a home, and children, and peace. Do you?

Aye, I do. I've asked God for these things. It's all for nothing if you don't have freedom.

That's just a dream William.

A dream? Just a . . . What we've been doing all this time? We've lived that dream.

While we the audience foresee the inevitable, Hamish delivers the third punch.

In Randall's original script, as the guard announces Wallace's approach to the meeting, the Bruce says, *He has got a brave heart*; the one and only time the term is used in the script. This dialogue was dropped from the final version.

As the Bruce angrily confronts his father for the last time, his father tells him,

> *Longshanks required Wallace. So did the nobles. That was the price of your crown.*

And so ends Act II. Wallace is captured and Scotland's resistance is seemingly at an end.

Act III

The End is only the Beginning

The scenes of Wallace's trial and execution shocked and moved audiences around the world. For those who did not know the Wallace story before *Braveheart*, it was almost inconceivable that this great man should be executed, let alone in this manner.

Wallace was put on trial in Westminster Hall, a crown of laurel on his head.

[51] The captive was not to be treated as a prisoner of war at the disposal of the executive; he was to be regularly tried on indictment as a subject of the King of England who had committed certain offences. He was not however permitted to plead to the indictment, because it was utterly adverse to the law of England that an outlawed person who had not been received to the king's peace should be permitted to plead. This method gained a judicial precedent for trying a native of Scotland before an English tribunal for offences committed in Scotland against a King of England and it completely stopped all inconvenient discussion as if the prisoner had been knocked on the head when he was taken.

[52] Even in his darkest hour Wallace still had the pride and dignity to deny he could ever be called a traitor, on the grounds that he had never sworn allegiance to the English king.

When the Princess visits Wallace in the cell before his execution, she orders the guard to let her in, saying,

The King will be dead in a month and his son is a weakling. Who do you think will rule this kingdom?

Edward I died two years after Wallace's execution. However, the Princess is right in that Edward's son was a weakling. She would later have him killed and take over the kingdom herself.

The cell is dirty, the prisoner sitting chained on the floor. The Princess, her love for him obvious, pleads with Wallace to swear allegiance and perhaps live. Wallace refuses.

Sir, I come to beg you to confess all and swear allegiance to the King, that he might show you mercy.

Will he show mercy to my country?

Mercy is to die quickly, perhaps live in the Tower. In time, who knows what could happen. If you can only live?

If I swear to him, then all that I am is dead already.

You will die. It will be awful.

Every man dies, not every man really lives.

Seeing that Wallace will be 'faithful unto death', the Princess tries to persuade him to drink a potion that will ease his pain. Wallace finally agrees because of her distress. When she leaves, he spits it out.

The Princess goes to see the dying King. In this room there is no love, only hatred; the impatient son's hatred of his dying father and Longshanks' hatred of Wallace, even now when Wallace is his prisoner. Longshanks' hatred of Wallace is his hatred of Scotland – Scotland, which, even at his death, still eludes his grasp.

The Princess begs for the life of Wallace to no avail.

Mercy . . . To you that word is as unfamiliar as love.

As they torture him, the *Braveheart* Wallace focuses on the face of an innocent child. *Blind Harry* has Wallace, a deeply religious man asking to be read to from his Psalter.

A psalter book, which he beseech'd a knight,
Lord Clifford, might be brought unto his sight.
Which done he caus'd a priest upon the place,
To hold it open straight before his face,
On which he look'd sometimes, his eyes up cast,
Religiously unto his very last.

At Wallace's death we revisit the main themes of the movie. Freedom, courage and love. Murron is there in his dream, waiting for him. Hamish and Stephen are there because of their courage, loyalty and love for him. Wallace dies for love of Scotland, with the courage he prayed for in his cell.

I am so afraid. Give me the strength to die well.

When Wallace sees the smiling Murron approaching him, we know death is near. For Wallace, love conquers pain and gives him the strength for his final defiant cry of

Freedom!

As Murron's wedding cloth drops from his hand, the future of Scotland must pass into the care of others.

The manner of the real Wallace's death sent shock waves around Scotland.

[53] The death of Wallace stands forth among the most violent ends which have a memorable place in history. Proverbially such acts belong to a policy that outwits itself. But the retribution has seldom come so quickly and so utterly in defiance of all human preparation and calculation, as here. Of all the bloody trophies sent to frighten a broken people into abject subjection, the bones had not yet been bared, ere they became tokens to deepen the wrath and strengthen the courage of a people arising to try the strength of the bands by which they were bound and, if possible, break them once and forever.

Edward managed to accomplish what he wanted least. He made Wallace more powerful in death than in life. As Nelson Mandela said, as he visited his former prison cell on the eve of the Millennium,

'The freedom flame can never be put down.'

Wallace's name has always been synonymous with freedom, both in Scotland and around the world.

Edward I died two years after Wallace at Burgh-on-Sands, in sight of Scotland, trying to lead another invasion. No sooner did he annihilate Wallace than The Bruce rose against him. Thinking Scotland in his grasp, Edward found it slipping away again, Wallace's life and death the catalyst for the events that followed.

The movie cannot end on Wallace's death, for his death was just the beginning of Scotland's fight for independence. Nigel Tranter ended his Wallace novel with the following words:

'William Wallace's dream came true seventeen years after he set himself to make it a reality. Who shall say that he lost his final battle?'

In *Braveheart*, Robert the Bruce continues the story:

After the beheading, William Wallace's body was torn to pieces. His head was placed on top of London Bridge, his arms and legs sent to the four corners of Britain as a warning. It did not have the effect that Longshanks planned. And I, Robert the Bruce, rode out to pay homage to the armies of the English King and accept his endorsement of my throne.

The Battle of Bannockburn took place in 1314, after nine years of war following Wallace's death. In the intervening years, the Bruce had gone from noble to being destitute, been excommunicated for his murder of the Comyn in 1306, and was crowned King of Scotland in March that year. The Bruce was a survivor. Once he had chosen his path, he remained on it through the hideous death or imprisonment of most of his family. But it was to be fourteen more years after the Battle of Bannockburn before a treaty with England acknowledged Scotland as independent with Bruce as Scotland's King.

We see The Bruce rising on his horse at Bannockburn and we see ranged behind him all the old familiar faces of the Wallace gang. Hamish has the Wallace sword and the Bruce fingers Murron's wedding cloth, the fate of Scotland now lying in his hands.

Wallace may not be there in body, but his spirit and soul are present.

As The Bruce calls the famous words

You have bled with Wallace, now bleed with me.

we are reminded of Burns' poem, 'Robert Bruce's March to Bannockburn'.

Scots wha hae wi' Wallace bled,
Scots wham Bruce has aften led,
Welcome to your gory bed
*   Or to victory!*
Now's the day, and now's the hour;
See the front o' battle lour;
See approach proud Edward's power
*   Chains and slaverie!*

Burns wrote 'Scots Wha Hae' using *Blind Harry* as inspiration for his hero. *Blind Harry* proved to be as inspirational for Randall Wallace as it had been for Burns,

'pouring a Scottish prejudice in (their) veins which will boil there until the floodgates of life shut in eternal rest.'

The Wallace sword rises, twisting and turning in the air, twisting and turning our emotions as the Scots chant the name of their hero for the third time.

Wallace, Wallace.

As the Scots run headlong to the slaughter, we hear the voice of Wallace completing Scotland's story:

In the year of our Lord 1314, patriots of Scotland charged the field of Bannockburn. They fought like warrior poets. They fought like Scotsmen. And won their freedom.

In analysing the script it would have been possible to identify additional significance in almost every exchange, but it was the portrayal of the characters that brought that dialogue to life. The reason why so many people went back to see *Braveheart* again and again is the layered texture of the drama. There is something in there for everyone.

On first showing, the complexity of the relationship of Bruce with his father is not appreciated, because we hate their scheming so much we don't pay attention. On further viewings, the dilemma of these characters becomes clear and the audience begins to appreciate the power of the acting involved. Patrick McGougan excelled as Edward I. The arrogance, power and single-mindedness of the man was frightening to behold. He and Wallace were worthy enemies. The mixture of famous faces and unknowns gave an edge to this production. Gibson wanted an unknown to play the part of Wallace but was required by the studios to star himself if he was to raise enough money to make the movie.

So *Braveheart* had money and expertise behind it, the dialogue was full of meaning for people today, the dramatic content was high, the acting polished and powerful, and the images evocative.

It would be possible to achieve all these things and yet not make a movie that people responded to the way they responded to *Braveheart*. People loved *Braveheart* because it had a heart and a soul. Each time they went to see it they emerged feeling stronger, either about themselves or if they were Scots about Scotland.

We need uncompromising heroes. Heroes that remind us what is important about life. Heroes that live out a dream and allow us, for a short time at least, to live that dream with them.

Chapter Eight

Braveheart A-Z

'Everything I needed to know about life I learned from Braveheart'

Airth Castle: Part of Airth Castle Hotel, near Falkirk, is known as The Wallace Tower. Blind Harry has Wallace storm this tower to rescue his Dunipace uncle. The Braveheart Convention of 2000 was based here.

Alba gu Brath: Scottish Gaelic for 'Scotland forever'. Mel Gibson shouts this at the end of the 'Sons of Scotland' speech before the Battle of Stirling. The meaning of what Mel shouts is one of the three most frequently asked questions in emails to the MacBraveHeart website.

Almondell Country Park: Some careful historical detective work has uncovered what appears to be the earliest memorial in Scotland dedicated to William Wallace. The carved stone is one of a pair to be found close to the Almondell Country Park, near Livingston in West Lothian. The William Wallace stone carries an inscription in Latin dedicating it to Wallace and the date 15 October 1784. The second stone carries an inscription in English dedicating the surrounding forest to Sir Simon Fraser, and the same date. Investigations by Russell Parker of the Battle of Falkirk Working Group have revealed that the stones were erected by the 11th Earl of Buchan, David Stewart Erskine and his wife Margaret Fraser of Frasersfield in Aberdeenshire, who owned the estate at that time. The Earl's fascination with William Wallace is well known, and he was responsible for the large statue of Wallace erected at Dryburgh in the Borders in 1814.

Further work was needed to track down the correct Sir Simon Fraser, as the name reoccurs regularly in the Fraser bloodline. However, there was one Sir Simon who was closely associated with Wallace. He was Sir Simon Fraser of Oliver and Neidpath, who fought by Wallace's side and at the side of Bruce. Sir Simon was captured by the English either at or soon after the Battle of Methven in June 1306 and, aged forty-nine, was sentenced to death by the same judges who sentenced Wallace and a number of other Scots. He was executed in the same barbaric way as Wallace had been a year earlier and his head was stuck on a spear on London Bridge beside that of Wallace. Although the stones are interesting in themselves, Russell's investigations have revealed that the Wallace Stone at Almondell is the earliest dated memorial to Wallace yet discovered. That honour had previously been held by the monument at Wallacestone near Falkirk, which carries a date of 1804. Although the Wallacestone monument is known to have replaced an earlier inscribed stone, no details of that have survived. The Almondell stone is thought to mark the spot from which Wallace and his men observed the English army at Kirkliston in July 1298, a few days before the Battle of Falkirk.

The Simon Fraser stone is located in the Country Park and is freely available. The William Wallace stone is located a few feet from the roadside at the north entrance to the park. It is on private land but is easily seen and photographed from the road.

Amadan: Scottish Gaelic for fool: (Expression used by MacGregor from the next glen when he brings his people to join the uprising in *Braveheart*).

Austin, Julie: Scottish actress who played the bride, carried away on her wedding night by the right of *prima nocte*. Her words to her husband before they take her away were silent, but she said, 'I love you. I'll be alright. I'll be okay.'

𝔅

Ballad *The Signal of the Bruce*: This ballad is taken from a book which has been in my family for many years: *Days at the Coast* by Hugh Macdonald, published in 1878 by Dunn & Wright, 176 Buchanan Street, Glasgow, Scotland in a New Edition. The original edition was completed by Hugh Macdonald in 1857. The book (in his own words) is: '*A series of sketches descriptive of the Frith of Clyde-its watering-places, its scenery, and its associations.*' In the chapter about Brodick and Lamlash on Arran, the author mentions the taking of Brodick Castle by the Bruce, talks about the 'King's Cave', and includes a wonderful ballad *The Signal of the Bruce* which includes the term 'brave hearts'.

'For weal or woe,' outspoke the Bruce,
'I sail for Scotia's shore;
With God's good aid, and yours, brave
    hearts,
To win my crown once more.'

'Here, in the face of Heaven, I draw
The sword that knows no sheath
Till Scotland stands erect and free,
Or I'm laid low in death.'

Oh! weel micht England rue that nicht,
Sair cause had she to mourn,
For the licht that gleaned o'er the Frith
    sae red
Was the dawn of Bannockburn.

The ballad is unattributed, but there is an implication that it was written by Hugh Macdonald himself.

Ballarat, Australia: Site of a Wallace monument sculpted by Percival Ball of Melbourne. Unveiled 24 May 1889.

Ballymore Eustace, County Kildare, Eire: The filming of the Battle of Falkirk in *Braveheart* took place here.

Baltimore Monument: In 1887 the Scots community in Baltimore, Maryland, USA, paid DW Stevenson to complete and ship to them a copy of the statue he had added to the exterior of the National Wallace Monument in Stirling. On 24 August 1997, the St Andrews Society and the city of Baltimore re-dedicated the monument for the city's 200th anniversary celebration.

Bannen, Ian: Respected Scottish actor who played The Bruce's father. Sent a fax to the first *Braveheart* convention in 1997 stating Scotland's debt to Randall Wallace and to Mel Gibson for *Braveheart*.

Died in a car accident, November 1999.

Bective Abbey, County Meath, Ireland: Used for cloisters scene between Isabella and her maid. Also the dungeon where Wallace was incarcerated prior to his execution.

Blair, John: John Blair was Wallace's personal Chaplain. Blind Harry claimed to have based his work on an original book in Latin, written by Thomas Gray, Parson of Liberton, and John Blair, confessor of Wallace, who after Wallace's death, entered Dunfermline Abbey as a monk. This Latin book had been commissioned by William Sinclair, Bishop of Dunkeld to send to the Pope. Some believe that this book could be in the Vatican Library to this day.

Blessington Lake, County Wicklow, Ireland: A seventeen-metre high tower was built to enact the drop from the window of Mornay's castle. Here Wallace spurs his horse through the window to jump into the 'moat' below. On the night that the scene was filmed the water level in the lake had dropped to less than two metres.

Blind Harry: c. 1440–c. 1493. The information known about Henry the Minstrel, biographer of Wallace, comes from the few entries in the Accounts of the Lord High Treasurer, listing payments to him for performances. Harry pointed out that no one paid for his composition. Harry's epic poem on Wallace is 11,877 stanzas, divided into twelve books, surviving only in one manuscript, copied in 1488 by John Ramsay and now in the National Library of Scotland. Luath Press, Edinburgh, reprinted the William Hamilton of Gilbertfield edition in 1998 and it shot to the top of the Scottish bestselling charts.

***Braveheart* – who is *Braveheart*?:** Is it Wallace or is it Robert the Bruce? In the original screenplay the Bruce jumps down from the table and says 'He has a brave heart' referring to Wallace. This was cut from the final shooting.

Braveheart **computer game:** Based on Mel Gibson's award-winning movie, Red Lemon's 1999 *Braveheart* game recreated the atmosphere and excitement of Scotland's legendary struggle for freedom against the English invaders.

Braveheart **Conventions:** International conventions of *Braveheart* enthusiasts. These took place in September 1997 at the Stirling Highland Hotel (on the morning of the devolution result in Scotland) and in August 2000 at Airth Castle Hotel, near Falkirk.

Braveheart **novel by Randall Wallace:** Published by Penguin Books Ltd 1995. Some of the extra scenes that feature in the novel were in the original screenplay, but were either deleted before shooting, or filmed and then omitted from the final cut.

Braveheart **sword:** A five-foot sword used by Mel Gibson in the movie *Braveheart* was sold for $170,000 (£116,000) at a charity auction of Hollywood memorabilia on Tuesday 6th March 2001.

The sword, one of a set used by Gibson when he played William Wallace in the film, was the top lot of the auction organised by Liam Neeson to benefit Unicef. 'I've never been in this sort of situation before,' said Neeson. 'But I'm told this is very, very high for an auction of this type.' The project was called Movie Action for Children and the proceeds were used to provide drugs to prevent mother-to-foetus transmissions of Aids in Africa.

Bruce movie: The movie *The Bruce* is available in the UK to hire or buy. It stars Oliver Reed, Brian Blessed and Michael van Wijk ('Wolf' from TV's Gladiators). It was made on a low budget during 1995, and it shows. Extras, who paid to be in the film, didn't want to be cast on the English side. Anyone who has seen *Braveheart* and is expecting a similar experience will likely be very disappointed. I couldn't really recommend it, other than for curiosity value.

Bruce's heart: King Robert died at Cardross on 7 July 1329. His body was buried in Dunfermline Abbey. At his request, his heart was taken on a Crusade by James Douglas. In battle against the Moors in Spain, Douglas was killed and the embalmed heart was returned to Scotland. It was buried in Melrose Abbey. Recently a new casket was created for the embalmed heart. In June 1998 a new commemorative stone was placed over the spot where his heart is interred. It says, in Scots, 'A noble hart may hae nae ease, gif freedom failye' – 'A noble heart may have no ease if freedom fail'.

Burns, Robert: Scotland's national poet. Born 25 January 1759, died 21 July 1796. Championed the cause of the common man. His song *Auld Lang Syne* is sung throughout the world, usually at New Year. A great admirer of William Wallace, he left a description of a long Sunday walk in the footsteps of Wallace 'to pay my respects to the "Leglen Wood" with as much devout enthusiasm as ever Pilgrim did to Lorretto, and as I explored every den and dell where I could suppose my heroic Countryman to have sheltered, I recollect

. . . that my heart glowed with a wish to be able to make a Song on him equal to his merits.'

Church, Tom: Following life-threatening open-heart surgery, Tom Church, a burly stonemason, was both physically and emotionally a reduced man. At this low point Tom watched the film *Braveheart*. So inspired was he by Wallace's patriotism and determination that Tom resolved to produce a sculpture that would capture the spirit of one of Scotland's greatest heroes. Work commenced in January 1996. For one thousand hours Tom chiselled two huge blocks of sandstone each weighing six tons. By May the impressive figure of Wallace had emerged from the stone echoing Tom's physical regeneration. On the 11 May 1996, the first anniversary of the cardiac surgery, the completion of the sculpture and Tom's return to good health were commemorated at a ceremony at his home town of Brechin, Angus. The National Wallace Monument was always considered by Tom to be the spiritual home for his creation. Unveiled by Nigel Tranter, the statue is at the time of writing located within a spear's throw of Wallace's brilliant victory over a far superior English force at the Battle of Stirling Bridge on 11 September 1297.

Cox, Brian: Played Wallace's Uncle Argyle in *Braveheart*. Very experienced Scottish character actor who has starred in many Hollywood movies including *Rob Roy*, *Adaptation*, *The Ring*, *The Bourne Supremacy* and *Troy*.

Curragh, The: The Battle of Stirling was filmed here. The Irish Government offered the use of the Irish Army Reserve as extras for the battle scenes. Some 1,400 soldiers became Scots and English infantry, cavalry and archers.

David R. Ross: The biker historian and Convener of the Society of William Wallace. Addressed both *Braveheart* conventions (1997 and 2000). His book *On the Trail of William Wallace* was published in 1999 by Luath Press, Edinburgh. Subsequent books include *On the Trail of Robert the Bruce*, *On the Trail of Bonnie Prince Charlie*, *A Passion for Scotland*, and *Desire Lines: a Scottish Odyssey*.

De Graeme, John: The nearest historical equivalent to Hamish in *Braveheart*. He features in Nigel Tranter's *The Wallace* as one of the few nobles who agreed to join Wallace's uprising. Blind Harry's *The Wallace* describes Sir John de Graeme as Wallace's closest and dearest friend. In the aftermath of William Wallace's defeat by King Edward I at the battle of Falkirk the bodies of two Scottish knights, Sir John de Graeme of Dundaff and Sir John Stewart of Bonkle, were interred in Falkirk Churchyard. Over the centuries the church-yard became a place of pilgrimage, especially after the publication of Blind Harry's *The Wallace* in the 16th century. Stewart lies under what appears to be the original 13th Century stone, while Sir John de Graeme's grave has been much modified over the years with the addition of an effigy and a series of ornate, engraved stones. One of the inscriptions reads :

> *Here lyse Sir John the Graeme,*
> *   baith wight and wise,*
> *Ane of the chiefs who saved*
> *   Scotland thrise,*
> *Ane better knight not to the*
> *   world was lent*
> *Nor was gude Graeme of truth*
> *   and hardiment*

Another, Latin, inscription translates as:

> *Of mind and courage stout*
> *Wallace's true Achates,*
> *Here lies Sir John the Graeme*
> *Felled by the English baties [dogs]*

In the 1860s a replica of Sir John de Graeme's sword was manufactured by Falkirk Iron Company and mounted on the uppermost stone of his grave and the whole tomb surrounded by an iron cupola. This sword has been broken for many years, probably since the last century, and the Battle of Falkirk Working Group commissioned a replacement, fitted to the gravestone in the year of the 700th anniversary of the Battle of Falkirk. The sword is based on photographs and drawings of the original, still held by the Auchterarder lodge of Freemasons in Perthshire. Falkirk Tourist Information Centre can be found in the town's Glebe Street, only a short walk from the churchyard.

Declaration of Arbroath: The Declaration of Arbroath was prepared as a formal Declaration of Independence. It was drawn up in Arbroath Abbey on 6 April 1320, most likely by the Abbot, Bernard de Linton, who was also the Chancellor of Scotland. The Declaration urged the Pope to see things from a Scottish perspective and not to take the English claim on Scotland seriously. It used strong words, indicating that without acceptance of the Scottish case the wars would continue and the resultant deaths would be the responsibility of the Pope. The Declaration was signed and bore the seals of 38 Scots Lords. It was conveyed to Rome and the Pope accepted the Scottish case. The words most quoted from it are:

'Yet if he (the King) should give up what he has begun, and agree to make us or our kingdom subject to the King of England or the English, we should exert ourselves at once to drive him out as our enemy and a subverter of his own rights and ours, and make some other man who was well able to defend us our King; for, as long as but a hundred of us remain alive, never will we on any conditions be brought under English rule. It is in truth not for glory, nor riches, nor honours that we are fighting, but for freedom – for that alone, which no honest man gives up but with life itself.'

Declaration of Independence: The Declaration of Independence of the Thirteen Colonies, made in Congress, 4 July 1776 rule. The Declaration of Arbroath is likely to have informed this document.

'We hold these truths to be self-evident, that all men are created equal, that they are endowed by their Creator with certain unalienable Rights, that among these are Life, Liberty and the pursuit of Happiness. — That to secure these rights, Governments are instituted among Men, deriving their just powers from the consent of the governed, — That whenever any Form of Government becomes destructive of these ends, it is the Right of the People to alter or to abolish it, and to institute new Government, laying its foundation on such principles and organising its powers in such form, as to them shall seem most likely to effect their Safety and Happiness.'

Dunsoughly Castle, County Dublin: Provided the exterior for Edinburgh Castle. For eight weeks prior to filming Tom Sanders and his team transformed the solitary stone structure into a busy, bustling castle with nine metre high battlements, a drawbridge, a great hall and peripheral 'A' frame houses with pitched roofs. Dunsoughly is on the flight path for Dublin's busy international airport and filming was constantly interrupted by planes taking off and landing.

Dryburgh Wallace Statue: This statue was one of the first monuments to be raised to Wallace in Scotland. The eleventh Earl of Buchan was very attached to the Dryburgh area and was himself buried at Dryburgh. He built a 260-foot suspension bridge over the river Tweed here and also commissioned a colossal statue of Wallace to be built. This statue was placed on its pedestal on 22 September 1814. It stands 21.5 feet high and is formed of red sandstone. When first raised it was painted white, but is now bare sandstone. The statue was designed by a Mr John Smith, a self-taught sculptor. He had copied its likeness from a supposedly authentic portrait that had been purchased in France by a Sir Philip Ainslie of Pilton. Wallace is represented in ancient Scottish armour, a shield hanging from his left hand, and leaning on a huge sword with his right. The statue was restored around 1990 by Graciela Ainsworth, one of Scotland's foremost sculpture conservators. She gave a very interesting talk on her work on this statue and with the 1821 Lanark Wallace statue at the Wallace Conference at the Smith Art Gallery and Museum in Stirling on 17 May, 1997. An urn in front of the statue bore what old accounts called 'a suitable inscription'. This is illegible in parts now due to erosion. The remaining words nevertheless convey the spirit of the piece. The statue can be found by following the Dryburgh road from St Boswells. Soon after the road crosses the river Tweed there is a side road on the left with a sign for the 'Wallace Statue'. The road is then signposted all the way to the car park for the statue. It is a five-minute walk through the woods from the car park to the statue. The sheer scale of the statue is only appreciated when standing close to it. The setting is absolutely magnificent, on the edge of a steep drop down towards the river Tweed. The spot is very peaceful with lovely views to the North and West, and is ideal for a picnic. The plaque on the front of the base of the statue has the inscription:

Erected by David Stuart
Erskine Earl of Buchan
WALLACE
GREAT PATRIOT HERO!
ILL REQUITED CHIEF!
Joannes Smith Sculptist

Due to the popularity of the statue, there were plans to enlarge the car park in 2005.

Edinburgh Castle Statues of Wallace and Bruce: Seen by Randall Wallace and his wife on a visit to Scotland. When he asked who Wallace was, the guard on the gate said, 'He is our greatest hero.'

These statues were erected by The Corporation of Edinburgh under Captain Hugh Reid's bequest 28 May 1929.

Elderslie: reputed to be Wallace's birthplace. Foundations of the family home are still there beside the monument to Wallace. At this place each year on the Saturday closest to the 23 August, the anniversary of Wallace's death in 1305, people gather to remember Wallace and the important part he played in the shaping of the Scottish nation.

Elspeth King's True Story of *Braveheart*: The booklet *Introducing William Wallace, Braveheart, The Life and Legacy of Scotland's Liberator*, by Elspeth King. Published to coincide with the 1997 exhibition on Wallace at the Smith Museum and Art Gallery in Stirling to commemorate the 700th anniversary of the Battle of Stirling Bridge.

'For seven hundred years, the story of Sir William Wallace has gripped the imagination of the people of Scotland both home and abroad. Over the centuries, he has been regarded without dispute as the heroic liberator of Scotland who made no compromises and sacrificed everything in his country's cause. Each new generation seeks to interpret his story and to honour him in different ways. Poets, songwriters, playwrights, sculptors and artists have regarded his life as a source of inspiration. Those struggling against oppression, tyranny, slavery and injustices both at home and abroad have looked back on his example as a liberator, and have drawn strength and lessons from it.'

Everything I needed to know about life I learned from *Braveheart*: Internationally popular poster made for the *Braveheart* convention of 1997. 'Some men are longer than others. Always remember the rocks. Don't stand on your head or your kilt will fly up. In order to find their equal the Irish are forced to talk to God. History is written by the winners. People don't follow titles, they follow courage. Be yourself. Wisdom before strength. Your heart is free, follow where it leads. Everyone dies but not everyone really lives. When love is true it lasts a lifetime and beyond. Prize peace above all things, and remember it cannot be bought with gold. If you must fight, then fight not for glory nor riches nor honours but for Freedom, which no one gives up but with life itself . . .'

Freedom's Sword: A Tale of the Days of Wallace and Bruce by Annie S Swan. First published in 1886. Annie Swan was born near Coldingham. She became a hugely popular writer and published over 100 books, mostly idealised romances. She died in 1943 at Gullane.

Gleeson, Brendan: Played the part of Hamish. Already an established and well-respected Irish actor, Brendan went on to play roles in many Hollywood movies after *Braveheart* including *Cold Mountain*, *Harry Potter & the Goblet of Fire*, *The Village* and *Troy*.

Glen Nevis filming location: Early scenes in *Braveheart* shot here were characterised by wonderful mountains and much rain and mud. The village and wooden fort were demolished on completion of filming.

Goodsir Smith Sydney's play *The Wallace*: Sydney Goodsir Smith, Poet, Playwright & Critic (1915-1975). Born in Wellington, New Zealand on 25 October 1915, Sydney Goodsir Smith's father was an army medical officer, and his mother was Scottish. He was educated in England at Malvern College before starting a medical degree at Edinburgh University, where his father was professor of forensic medicine. Hating anatomy, he abandoned this degree and went to Oxford instead to study at Oriel College. Thereafter he returned to Scotland, whose culture and history he enthusiastically embraced, and which was to form the basis of all his subsequent work.

Now viewed by some as an equal with Hugh MacDiarmid as a poet of the Scottish Renaissance, Goodsir Smith quickly adopted Scots for his poetry, appropriating many archaisms and delving deep into the late medieval tradition of Scottish makars for stylistic inspiration. His play, *The Wallace*, was broadcast on the Scottish Service on 30 November 1959 and performed at the Edinburgh Festival of 1960 and again in an outdoor production at the 2001 Edinburgh Festival Fringe. In the play Wallace's wife is called Mirren. In the introduction to the book of the play (1960) one quote from a leading article on the Nuremberg trials and executions in the Manchester Guardian 16 Oct 1946 runs . . . 'Could any Englishman doubt that justice was done, if brutally, when Wallace was executed?'

Grave: did Wallace have one? No grave for Wallace. He was hung, drawn and quartered. His head was stuck on London Bridge and the four parts of his body were distributed throughout the kingdom (Newcastle, Berwick, Stirling and Perth) as a warning to the Scots not to defy the will of Edward 1. lacking a grave, Wallace was canonised by his people and they honoured places and objects associated with him.

H

Hamilton of Gilbertfield: A translation and adaptation of *Blind Harry's Wallace* issued in 1722 as 'A New Edition of the Life and Heroic Actions of the Renou'd Sir William Wallace, General and Governor of Scotland'.

Historical accuracy: Most people who claimed the film was inaccurate had never even heard of *Blind Harry's Wallace*, showing how little they knew of their own history.

J

Internet Movie Database: *Braveheart* is in 84th place in the top 250 films of all time, ten years after its release.

K

Kinfauns Castle statues: James Stewart and his younger brother were granted the land of Kinfauns in 1382 by Robert II, King of Scotland. James, along with other duties, was the keeper of Edinburgh Castle. Upon the death of the heir-less James Stewart, the lands reverted to the crown, after which they became part of the lands of Sir Thomas Charteris, related to the Earl of Wemyss. The first Thomas Charteris was also known as Thomas de Longueville (the Red Reiver in *Blind Harry*) and the Frenchman was the first nobleman to follow Robert the Bruce at the capture of Perth in 1313. For his bravery and devotion he was rewarded with lands in the Perth area.

The statues of Wallace and Bruce were put up at the same time as the present castle was built in 1822. These statues standing in the garden were believed to have been carved by a stonemason from Dumfries.

Lake of Menteith: Only lake in Scotland (the rest are called lochs). Called by the English term 'lake' because Sir John Menteith, Edward's sheriff in Dumbarton, was the traitor who handed over Wallace.

Lanark Wallace statue: Lanark has always been proud of its Wallace associations and in 1821, Robert Forrest (1789-1852) presented a Wallace statue which was mounted on the façade of St Nicholas Church in the heart of the town. The monument is the focal point for the annual Lanimer celebrations, which begin and end there. Nearby is the remaining stone of Wallace's house.

MacAulish: Scottish Gaelic for 'Son of Wallace'. An echo of a scene in the epic movie El Cid. In *Braveheart*, chanted at Wallace after he slays the Sheriff of Lanark who had murdered his wife. This signals the start of the uprising. They have chosen him to lead them. There is no way back now.

MacBraveHeart: Name of the webpage dedicated to the movie *Braveheart*, bringing a unique Scottish perspective on the film.

Make-a-Wish Foundation: An American charity dedicated to granting the wishes of seriously ill children. The foundation contacted the MacBraveHeart webpage and asked that we meet one of their children whose greatest wish was to come to Scotland and learn more about William Wallace.

A BRAVE HEART INDEED

American 13 year old Richard Schwenning (Barberton, Ohio) who was fighting for his life as he battled against a killer: Burkitt's Lymphoma visited Scotland to walk in the footsteps of his greatest hero: William Wallace. On Halloween the boy was even able to wear Mel Gibson's *Braveheart* costume to a party at Airth Castle in Stirlingshire. The visit to Scotland by Richard and his family was made possible by the Make-A-Wish Foundation.

Marceau, Sophie: Though well known in Europe, it wasn't until her role as Princess Isabelle in Mel Gibson's *Braveheart* that North American audiences became aware of her. *Braveheart* was her 16th feature film.

McCormack, Catherine: Played Wallace's wife, Murron, in the movie. This was her breakthrough part. She has starred in many films since then including Spy Game which Brad Pitt and Robert Redford. TV work includes starring as Queen Elizabeth I in BBC production, Gunpowder, Treason and Plot.

Miller, Hugh: *Scenes and Legends of the North of Scotland*. Hugh Miller was born in Cromarty in 1802. His pioneering work in the field of geology was recognised throughout the world, while in Britain his writing on many subjects made him one of the best known of Victorian literary figures. Miller, researching the history of Cromarty discovered a story of Wallace.

'Somewhat more than four miles to the south of Cromarty . . . there is a little wooded eminence. Like the ridge which it overtops, it sweeps gradually towards the east until it terminates in an abrupt precipice that overhangs the sea, and slopes upon the west into a marshy hollow, known to elderly people of the last age and a very few of the present as Wallace-slack (ravine).' Here the local story goes, Wallace surprised and defeated six hundred English, en route from Ardersier to Easter Ross. Wallace then raised the English siege on Cromarty castle.

Nelson, Sandy: Played William's brother John, who was killed with his father at the battle of Loudon Hill. Sandy is also a musician and successful stand up comedian.

Pap of Glencoe: The hilltop where Mel Gibson is seen running along a path to the summit cairn.

R B Cunninghame Graham: A leading Scottish Nationalist and socialist. He was president of the second Scottish Home Rule Association and was elected president of the National Party of Scotland following its formation in 1928. Cunninghame Graham also served as first president of the Scottish chapter of PEN, which Hugh MacDiarmid founded in 1927. He admired Wallace:

> Wallace made Scotland; he is Scotland; he is the symbol of all that is
> best and purest and truest and most
> heroic in our national life. You cannot
> figure to yourself Scotland without Wallace. So long as grass grows green
> or water runs, or whilst the mist curls
> through the corries of the hills, the memory of Wallace will live.

Robin Hood connection: Not dissimilar story to William Wallace. Both had a love called Marion. Both were bowmen. Both fought against the ruling order. Both hid out in the woods. Both had a love of the common man. In

Wyntown's *Scottish Chronicle* (about 1420) both Robin Hood and Little John are ascribed to the year 1283. In Fordun and Bower's *Scotichronicon*, a fifteenth century work, these two outlaws are said to have lived in 1266. There can be little doubt the stories influenced one another.

Robinson, James: Played the part of young William in the movie. Attended both *Braveheart* conventions. In the immediate aftermath of *Braveheart* he did not want to pursue an acting career but later studied drama.

Saint Bart's Hospital Wallace plaque in London: The plaque near Smithfield where Wallace was executed has the following inscription.

TO THE IMMORTAL MEMORY OF
SIR WILLIAM WALLACE
SCOTTISH PATRIOT BORN AT ELDERSLIE
RENFREWSHIRE CIRCA 1270 AD WHO FROM
THE YEAR 1296 FOUGHT DAUNTLESSLY
IN DEFENCE OF HIS COUNTRY'S LIBERTY AND
INDEPENDENCE IN THE FACE OF FEARFUL
ODDS AND GREAT HARDSHIP BEING
EVENTUALLY BETRAYED AND CAPTURED
BROUGHT TO LONDON AND PUT TO DEATH
NEAR THIS SPOT ON THE
23RD AUGUST 1305

HIS EXAMPLE AND HEROISM AND DEVOTION
INSPIRED THOSE WHO CAME AFTER HIM
TO WIN VICTORY FROM DEFEAT AND HIS
MEMORY REMAINS FOR ALL TIME A SOURCE
OF PRIDE HONOUR AND INSPIRATION
TO HIS COUNTRYMEN

DICO TIBI VERUM LIBERTAS OPTIMA RERUM
NUNQUAM SERVILI SUB NEXU VIVITO FILI
(Latin for *Freedom is best, I tell thee true of all things to be won*
Then never live within the bond of slavery, my son.
Attributed to Wallace's uncle, priest of Dunipace.)

BAS AGUS BUAIDH
(Gaelic for *Death and Victory*)

Scotland's Liberator Exhibition: An exhibition commemorating the 700th anniversary of the Battle of Stirling Bridge (1297 – 1997) held at the Stirling Museum and Art Gallery from 1 April to 15 December 1997 to celebrate the life and legacy of William Wallace. Elspeth King, the museum's curator, drew together paintings and artefacts from public and private collections in Britain, including those treasured by generations because of their association with Wallace. The exhibition looked at how the story of Wallace was handed down, how hundred of places throughout Scotland were given his name. How his deeds were celebrated by some of the great poets such as Wordsworth (and Burns).

> . . . I would relate
> How Wallace fought for Scotland; left the name
> Of 'Wallace' to be found like a wild flower
> All over his dear country; left the deeds
> Of Wallace, like a family of ghosts
> To people the steeps rocks and river banks
> Her natural sanctuaries, with a local soul
> Of Independence and stern Liberty.
>
> William Wordsworth

At this exhibition there was a special display of a selection of the thousands of emails sent to the MacBraveHeart website from around the world showing the international impact of *Braveheart* and the Wallace story.

Scottish Chiefs: A novelised version of Wallace's life by Jane Porter, first published in 1810. She also used *Blind Harry* as a major source, stating in her Preface, 'The melancholy circumstance which first excited him to draw his sword for Scotland, although it may be thought too much like the creation of modern romance, is recorded as a fact in the old poem of *Blind Harrie*.'

The novel begins thus:

'Bright was the summer of 1296. The war which had desolated Scotland was then at an end. Ambition seemed satiated; and the vanquished, after having passed under the yoke of their enemy, concluded they might wear their chains in peace. Such were the hopes of those Scottish noblemen who, early in the preceding spring, had signed the bond of submission to a ruthless conqueror, purchasing life at the price of all that makes life estimable – liberty and honour . . . William Wallace retired to the glen of Elderslie. Withdrawn from the world, he hoped to avoid the sight of oppressions he could not redress, and the endurance of injuries beyond his power to avenge.'

Scottish National Party: In the aftermath of the release of *Braveheart*, the SNP used Mel's photograph on a leaflet exhorting Scots to vote for independence. Membership of the party increased during this time.

Stephen of Ireland: Played by Scot, David O'Hara. Humorous character, much loved in the movie. A companion of Wallace in *Blind Harry's Wallace*.

> But Wallace grieving for his native land,
> Resolv'd what store of men he might to raise,
> To combat in the field for Scotland's praise.
> Stephen of Ireland, exil'd from his home,
> Did there into a league with Wallace come.
> So did Faudron, a man of dreadful size,
> Of threatening aspect, and iniquious eyes;

Spartacus: Another favourite film of Gibson's which influenced his realisation of the Wallace story. *Spartacus* and *Braveheart* have much in common, both heroes fighting for freedom and both enduring terrible deaths at the hands of the ruling elite. The novel *Spartacus* was written by the Scot Lewis Grassic Gibbon writing under his real name, James Leslie Mitchell.

St Nicholas Church, County Meath, Eire: Built in the 12th century it was dressed up to become Westminster Abbey for the *Braveheart* wedding of Prince Edward to Princess Isabella.

Sunset Song **by Lewis Grassic Gibbon:** The quintessential Scottish book set in the Mearns in Aberdeenshire is the first part of the trilogy, *A Scots Quair*. Wallace appears early in the Prelude, *The Unfurrowed Field*. 'And the great-grandson of Cospatric, he joined the English against a certain Wallace, and when Wallace next came marching up from the southlands Kinraddie and the other folk of that time they got them into Dunottar Castle that stands out in the sea beyond Kineff, well-builded and strong . . . But Wallace came through the Howe right swiftly and he heard of Dunottar and laid siege to it and it was a right strong place and he had but small patience with strong places. So, in the dead of night, when the thunder of the sea drowned the noise of his feint, he climbed the Dunottar rocks and was over the wall, he and the vagabond Scots, and they took Dunottar and put to the slaughter the noble folk gathered there, and all the English, and spoiled them of their meat and gear and marched away.'

Tartan: When the Apollo spacecraft landed on the moon Allan Bean, one of the crew, reverentially laid a swatch of MacBean tartan on the moon's surface. Allan Bean's gesture was understood and applauded. Tartan is a symbol of kinship and belonging in Scotland, and a badge of identity recognised all over the world. The designers of *Braveheart* insisted on using tartan for this very reason.

Thistle National Flower of Scotland: The 'gift of a thistle' scene would have been tricky in reality, given the prickly nature of the plant.

Trim Castle, Eire: This was the first time a film production crew was allowed to build on one of Ireland's foremost medieval monuments. The exterior of King John's castle in Trim, County Meath was transformed into the fortified English town of York with the addition of seven-ton gates and the replacement of wooden buttresses. Inside the walls, the London set was created.

V

Video store *Bravehearts* (cardboard): The cardboard cut out of Mel Gibson as Wallace became a highly desirable commodity, changing hands for large sums of money. As *Braveheart* was not a merchandise movie, souvenirs were hard to find.

W

Wallace liqueur: Wallace Single Malt Scotch Whisky Liqueur originated in the Highlands and is made by The Wallace Malt Liqueur Company, Deanston, Perthshire, Scotland. The label says:

'The Wallace' derives its name from the great William Wallace – The Guardian of Scotland – who fought his most famous battle in 1297 at Stirling Bridge, only a few miles from where the whisky is distilled at Deanston. The soft flavour of local herbs through the single malt makes this liqueur truly unique. In 1997 this liqueur got the Gold Winner new product award for best new drink from Scotland.

It tastes nice too.'

Wallace marmalade: Mathiesons' 'The Wallace Range' derives its name from Sir William Wallace, the famous Scottish hero and guardian of Scotland, whose exploits were portrayed in the highly acclaimed movie *Braveheart*.

Wallace's Tower, Tower of London: The place where Wallace was imprisoned in the Tower of London.

Wallace Clan Trust: Randall Wallace pays tribute to the help given by Seoras and Pamella Wallace when he was researching and writing *Braveheart*. Clan Wallace also featured widely in the battle scenes of *Braveheart*.

Westminster Hall, London: If you can get invited inside, you can stand in Westminster Hall and look up at the same windows Wallace saw as they condemned him, as Nelson Mandela did. When told where he was standing he said he was pleased. He had seen the movie.

Wallace's Well: The area around Robroyston near Glasgow was once dotted with wells, and Wallace's Well is the only one remaining.

It was at a farm in the area on 5 August, 1305, that Wallace was betrayed and captured by Scottish lord Sir John Monteith and sent to the Tower of London, where he was later hanged, drawn and quartered. The monument marking the building where Wallace was betrayed was erected in 1900, shortly after the house fell into ruin. Sir Walter Scott removed a number of roof beams and had them carved into chairs for his house at Abbotsford in the Borders.

Wallace's Well was rebuilt sometime in the 19th century, but both it and the monument sit isolated on a small country road. There is no parking or sign-posting. David R. Ross (the biker historian) said Randall Wallace visited Robroyston when he was researching *Braveheart*. He was said to be moved by the simplicity of the well and gave his backing to the campaign to have it turned into a national monument.

A spokeswoman for Glasgow City Council said: 'We decided against signage due to the unsuitability of the roads. We regularly inspect the monument and include it on our tourism website.' (*The Scotsman* newspaper, September 2003)

***Wallace's Women*:** A two-act comedy-drama, *Wallace's Women* was written specially for the 1997 Wallace 700th anniversary celebrations by Margaret McSeveney and Elizabeth Roberts. The play brings to the fore for the first time the unsung contribution of the women in Scottish history – in this case Wallace's mother, wet-nurse, girlfriend and wife, a healer who saved his life and a Frenchwoman. The play, written in Scots, centres on the celebration of the Celtic pagan feast of Beltaine on May 1st in two momentous years: 1296 and 1297. There are twelve characters in the play for six female actors.

Lin saw the play performed at the Smith Museum & Art Gallery in Stirling on Sunday 2 November, 1997. Her review follows:

'I loved *Wallace's Women*. These women were gutsy and funny and strong and loveable. I wanted to be all of them. I wanted to sit with them and gossip about William Wallace. I wanted to get drunk with them and dance at the feast of Beltaine. This was real history told by the women who knew Wallace, from birth through marriage and fatherhood to death. Watching and listening to these women made me understand what Wallace must have meant to the ordinary people of Scotland. This play marks an important point in the history of Scotland. It was written to mark the 700th commemorative year of Wallace's exploits in Lanark and at Stirling Bridge. It is an excellent example of the richness of our cultural and literary heritage, but it is more than that. The play celebrates the unique part played by the largely forgotten women, women without whom Scotland would never have had a William Wallace, for it was they who nurtured the boy and created the man.'

Weir, Andrew: Played young Hamish in the movie. Attended both *Braveheart* Conventions. Went on to play UK stage and TV roles.

Woad: The herb vitrium or woad. Classical scholars record north Britons as painting their faces, usually blue. Used to frighten opponents and show what side you were on. Not dissimilar to football fans now.

X-Wild: Braveheart lyrics by X-Wild. Found at Xwild-lyrics.wonderlyrics.com

Yolande: Wife of Alexander III, who he was returning to, when he fell off the cliff.

Young Murron: Mhairi Calvey played the part. She is currently studying drama and is in regular contact with other members of the *Braveheart* cast.

Zulunation.com: Webpages dedicated to the Zulu Nation. *Braveheart* features as one of their 'movies that are dropping knowledge'.

circa 1270	Birth of William Wallace.
19 March 1286	King Alexander of Scotland dies without an heir.
6 May 1291	King Edward I of England declares his overlordship of Scotland as part of his process of adjudication in the dispute as to who should become King of Scotland.
17 November 1292	Edward I judges John Balliol to be the rightful King of Scotland.
1293-1294	Edward I takes every opportunity to increase his influence over Scotland, making it impossible for King John to rule effectively.
23 October 1295	Scottish treaty with King Philip of France, as a prelude to war (jointly) with England.
1 March 1296	English army musters at Newcastle.
26 March 1296	Scottish army under Earl of Buchan raids Carlisle area.
30 March 1296	Edward I sacks Berwick.
27 April 1296	Scottish army heavily defeated by English army under John de Warrene at Battle of Dunbar.
May–June 1296	Edward I's army progresses through Scotland unopposed. Stone of Destiny is taken from Scone and sent south.
10 July 1296	John Balliol surrenders his kingdom to Edward I at Stracathro church-yard.
28 August 1296	Edward I holds Parliament at Berwick. Scots nobles sign the Ragman's Roll.

April or early May 1297	Wallace kills Heselrig, Sheriff of Lanark, and begins his rebellion.
May 1297	Andrew de Moray raises his standard at Ormonde Castle by Avoch, beginning a rebellion in the north.
11 September 1297	Scottish army, under the command of William Wallace and Andrew de Moray, defeats English army at the Battle of Stirling Bridge.
circa October 1297	Wallace knighted, and made Guardian of Scotland.
October-November 1297	Wallace raids northern England.
21 July 1298	Scottish army, led by Wallace, is defeated by the army of Edward I at the Battle of Falkirk. Wallace resigns the Guardianship of Scotland soon after.
August 1299	Wallace leaves Scotland, likely bound for Norway, then France.
7 November 1300	King Philip of France writes a letter instructing his representatives in Rome to assist Wallace on his arrival there.
1303	Wallace back in Scotland.
3 August 1305	Wallace is captured at Robroyston near Glasgow.
23 August 1305	Wallace is executed at Smithfield in London.
February 1306	Robert the Bruce stabs John Comyn in Greyfriars Church in Dumfries, and seizes the Scottish throne.
7 July 1307	Edward I dies at Burgh-on-Sands.
23-24 June 1314	Scottish army, under King Robert the

	Bruce, wins a decisive victory against the army of Edward II at the Battle of Bannockburn.
17 March 1328	Treaty of Edinburgh (ratified at Northampton on 4 May) brings peace with England and independence for Scotland.
7 June 1329	Robert the Bruce dies at Cardross.
circa 1477	Blind Harry's *Wallace* written.
1505	King James IV of Scotland has the sword of Wallace re-hilted.
24 March 1603	Union of the Crowns on the death of Queen Elizabeth I. James VI of Scotland succeeds to the throne of England. Scotland and England now have a single monarch.
22 August 1642	Charles I raises his standard at Nottingham. English Civil War begins.
1 January 1651	Charles II crowned King of Scots at Scone. The last coronation to take place in Scotland.
16 January 1707	Treaty of Union is passed in the Scottish Parliament, it meets for the last time on 25 March 1707. Scotland and England are now governed from a single Parliament in London.
6 September 1715	Earl of Mar unfurls the standard of the 'Old Pretender'. First Jacobite uprising begins.
1722	Blind Harry's *Wallace* translated into a contemporary form of Scots

	language by William Hamilton of Gilbertfield.
19 August 1745	Bonnie Prince Charlie raises his standard at Glenfinnan. Second Jacobite uprising begins.
25 January 1759	Robert Burns, Scotland's National Poet, born.
1 July 1782	Proscription Act repealed. The wearing of tartan and the carrying of weapons (banned since the '45 Rebellion) allowed again.
15 October 1784	Lord Buchan erects memorial stone to Wallace at Almondell.
1794	Robert Burns's *Scots Wha Hae* published.
1809	Jane Porter's *The Scottish Chiefs* published.
1810	Wallacestone memorial erected by Falkirk colliers.
1814	Lord Buchan erects statue of Wallace at Dryburgh.
1819	Wallace statues erected in High Street, Ayr.
1828	Wallace Tower and statue erected in Ayr.
28 June 1838	Queen Victoria, descendant of King Robert the Bruce, is crowned at Westminster Abbey.
24 May 1852	Robert Cunninghame Graham born. Co-founder of the Scottish Labour Party, he was elected first president of the Scottish National Party.
1855	Barnwell Monument to the burning

	by Wallace of the Barns of Ayr is erected.
June 1861	A crowd of 70,000 attend, as the foundation stone is laid for the National Wallace Monument on Abbey Craig.
1869	National Wallace Monument at Stirling built.
1886	*Freedom's Sword*, Annie S Swan's romantic novel of the days of Wallace and Bruce is published.
25 June 1887	Wallace statue unveiled at the National Monument in Stirling.
1888	Wallace statue by WG Stevenson erected in Aberdeen.
17 November 1888	Wallace Sword moved from Dumbarton Castle to the National Wallace Monument.
24 May 1889	Wallace statue at Ballarat, Australia, unveiled.
1929	Cairn erected in Leglen Wood to commemorate the visits of Robert Burns in the footsteps of Wallace.
November 1936	Wallace Sword stolen by nationalists. Recovered some months later at Bothwell Bridge.
April 1956	Memorial plaque installed on wall of St Bart's hospital in London, at the site of Wallace's execution.
30 November 1959	Sydney Goodsir Smith's play *The Wallace* is broadcast on the BBC Scottish Service.
17 February 1975	Nigel Tranter's novel *The Wallace* published.

1983	Randall Wallace visits Edinburgh Castle and sees statues of Wallace and Bruce.
1986	Andrew Fisher's life of Wallace published. Last pre-*Braveheart* biography.
Spring/Summer 1994	*Braveheart* filmed in Scotland and Ireland.
24 May 1995	*Braveheart* opens in USA cinemas.
1 June 1995	*Braveheart* novel by Randall Wallace published.
3 September 1995	*Braveheart* European premiere in Stirling.
November 1995	MacBraveHeart website goes online. (http://www.braveheart.co.uk)
25 March 1996	*Braveheart* wins 5 Oscars.
April 1996	*Braveheart* wins *Empire Magazine* UK readers poll as the best movie of the year.
June 1996	Regular *Braveheart* cinema showings in Scotland finally end.
30 November 1996	Stone of Destiny is returned to Scotland.
1 April 1997	'Scotland's Liberator' exhibition opens at Smith Museum and Art Gallery in Stirling.
11 September 1997	Referendum for re-establishment of a Scottish Parliament, held on 700th anniversary of the Battle of Stirling Bridge.
12–14 September 1997	First *Braveheart* Convention, based at Stirling, Scotland.
1998	Luath Press edition of Hamilton of

	Gilbertfield's *Blind Harry's Wallace* is published.
7 January 1999	First UK terrestrial TV showing of *Braveheart*. This sparked a two-week *Braveheart* debate in Scottish newspaper letters pages.
12 February 1999	DJ Sakin's *Protect Your Mind (For the Love Of A Princess)* trance tune featuring the theme from *Braveheart* is released.
19 February 1999	David R. Ross's book *On the Trail of William Wallace* launched by Luath Press.
May 1999	*Braveheart* computer game, developed by Glasgow company Red Lemon, is launched.
1 July 1999	Royal opening of re-established Scottish Parliament. *Braveheart* theme music opens and closes the BBC television coverage. Commemorative *Braveheart* video boxed set released.
October 1999	UK *Empire Magazine* readers vote *Braveheart* as one of the top 100 movies of all time.
6 April 2000	American Scottish Foundation revives the Wallace Award.
8 May 2000	First History Channel showing of 'True Story of *Braveheart*'.
18 –20 August 2000	Second *Braveheart* Convention, based at Airth, Scotland.
29 August 2000	*Braveheart* DVD released.
March 2001	Mel Gibson donates one of his

	Braveheart swords to a charity auction. It is bought by Celtic Football Club director Dermot Desmond for £116,000.
5 April 2001	Sir Sean Connery receives the William Wallace Award on Capitol Hill.
August 2001	Sir Sydney Smith's play *The Wallace* is performed outdoors at the Edinburgh International Festival.
November 2001	UK *Empire Magazine* publishes results of a readers poll for the 50 best movies of all time, showing *Braveheart* at No. 31.
20 October 2003	*Braveheart* gets a special screening at the Academy of Motion Picture Arts and Sciences in Beverly Hills, as part of a '75 Years of Best Picture Winners' series of showings. Randall Wallace, Bruce Davey, Tom Saunders and other crew members are present.
March 2004	UK *Empire Magazine* publishes results of their 2003 readers poll for the 100 best movies of all time. *Braveheart* features on the list again.
9 October 2004	Official Opening of the Scottish Parliament building at Holyrood. Phil Horwood, who works in the security department, wears a *Braveheart* tartan kilt as he carries The Ceremonial Mace into the new debating chamber.
March 2005	An *Empire Magazine* feature by film critic Patrick Peters, where he

	nominates *Braveheart* as the Worst Best Film ever, sparks another two-week newspaper letters debate in Scotland.
2 April 2005	*Braveheart* screenwriter Randall Wallace is honoured with an invitation to be Grand Marshall of the 2005 Tartan Day Parade in New York.
23 July 2005	Opening of The Face of William Wallace exhibition at Stirling Smith Art Gallery and Museum.
3 August 2005	David R. Ross sets off in his 'Walk for Wallace' from Robroyston, to arrive in London on 22 August 2005.
23 August 2005	700th Anniversary of the execution of William Wallace. Commemorative Service held at St Bartholomew the Great, London.
10 September 2005	Wallace and Scotland Conference at Stirling Smith Art Gallery and Museum.
24–25 September 2005	Celebrating Scotland's Heroes: Reputation and New Perspective Conference at University of Stirling.

1   CUNNINGHAME GRAHAM, RB.
2   BURTON, John Hill. Historiographer Royal for Scotland.
    The History of Scotland. (Edinburgh and London 1873).
3   HANSEN, Doug. 19 June 1999.
4   SMART, A. *Braveheart by The Big Issue in Scotland.*
5   GIBSON, Mel. *Braveheart: A Filmmaker's Passion* (2000).
6   ibid.
7   ibid.
8   ibid.
9   ibid.
10 McCORMACK, Catherine. *Braveheart: A Filmmaker's
    Passion* (2000).
11 GIBSON, Mel. *Braveheart: A Filmmaker's Passion* (2000).
12 Internet review of the film on 01 June 1995.
13 NATHAN, Ian. British edition of *Empire* magazine, October
    1995.
14 ibid.
15 http://desert.net/filmvault, 01-06-95.
16 NORTON, Dr Graham, Edinburgh University, Scottish
    Connection BBC Scotland 12/01/99.
17 TRANTER, Nigel. *The Wallace*, (Edinburgh 1975).
18 McARTHUR, Colin. *Braveheart and the Scottish Aesthetic
    Dementia. Screening the Past: Film and the Representation of
    History.* (1998).
19 McKEE, Robert. *Story.* (London 1998).
20 ibid.
21 EDENSOR, Tim. *Reading Braveheart: Representing and
    Contesting Scottish Identity. Scottish Affairs,* no 21, autumn
    1997.
22 REESE, Peter. *Wallace* (Edinburgh 1998).
23 KING, Elspeth, Introduction to *Blind Harry's Wallace*
    (Edinburgh 1998)
24 DOUGLASS, Frederick. Rochester New York – April 1947
    Address to a Burns Supper. (Widely available on the net).
25 MEIKLE, Henry, His Majesty's Historiographer in Scotland.
    Scotland. (Edinburgh 1947).

[26] McKEE, Robert. *Story*. (London 1998).

[27] REESE, Peter. *Wallace* (Edinburgh 1998).

[28] TRANTER, Nigel. *The Wallace*, (Edinburgh 1975).

[29] Heritage of Britain, 1975.

[30] Declaration of Arbroath.

[31] The Declaration of Independence.

[32] DAVIES, *Domination and Conquest*.

[33] Hamilton, William, of Gilbertfield *Blind Harry's Wallace* (Luath Press, Edinburgh, 1998).

[34] SIMPSON, W. Douglas. *Scottish Castles*, HMSO. (Edinburgh 1959).

[35] REESE, Peter. *Wallace* (Edinburgh 1998).

[36] BURTON, John Hill. Historiographer Royal for Scotland. *The History of Scotland*. (Edinburgh and London 1873).

[37] MACKAY, James. *William Wallace Braveheart*. (Edinburgh 1995).

[38] REESE, Peter. *Wallace* (Edinburgh 1998).

[39] MACKENZIE, Alex. *The Highland Clearances*. (Scotland).

[40] REESE, Peter. *Wallace* (Edinburgh 1998).

[41] ibid.

[42] John of Fordrun, Scottish chronicler.

[43] REESE, Peter. *Wallace* (Edinburgh 1998).

[44] ibid.

[45] ibid.

[46] ibid.

[47] ibid.

[48] ibid.

[49] ibid.

[50] BURTON, John Hill. Historiographer Royal for Scotland. *The History of Scotland*. (Edinburgh and London 1873).

[51] REESE, Peter. *Wallace* (Edinburgh 1998).

[52] ibid.

[53] BURTON, John Hill. Historiographer Royal for Scotland. *The History of Scotland*. (Edinburgh and London 1873).

Further Reading

Novels

Wallace, Margaret. *William Wallace – Champion of Scotland* (Goblinshead, Musselburgh 1999)

Wallace, Randall. *Braveheart* (Simon & Schuster, New York 1995, Signet, London 1995)

Tranter, Nigel. *The Bruce Triology* (Hodder & Stoughton, London 1969-71)
The Wallace (Hodder & Stoughton, London 1975)

Epic Poems

Barbour, John. *The Bruce* (Mercat Press, Edinburgh, reprinted 1996)

Hamilton, William, of Gilbertfield. *Blind Harry's Wallace* (Luath Press, Edinburgh 1998), introduced by Elspeth King

Biographies

Fisher, Andrew. *William Wallace* (John Donald, Edinburgh, 1986)

Ferguson, James. *William Wallace, Guardian of Scotland* (Aeneas MacKay, Stirling, 1948)

King, Elspeth. *An Introduction to Scotland's Liberator, William Wallace 1297-1997* (Firtree Publishing, Fort William, 1997)

Smart, Alan. *Wallace, Scotland's Braveheart* (Big Issue in Scotland, 1997)

Reese, Peter. *Wallace, A Biography* (Canongate, Edinburgh, 1996)

Guides

Ross, David R. *On the Trail of Robert the Bruce* (Luath Press, 1999)
On the Trail of William Wallace (Luath Press, 1999)

History

Barrow, G.W.S. *Robert Bruce & the Community of the Realm of Scotland* (Edinburgh University Press, Edinburgh 1998)

Reese, Peter. *Bannockburn* (Canongate, Edinburgh 2000)

Watson, Fiona. *Under the Hammer – Edward I and Scotland* (Tuckwell Press, Midlothian 1998)

Blind Harry's Wallace

William Hamilton of Gilbertfield

Introduced by Elspeth King

ISBN 0 946487 33 2 PBK £8.99

The original story of the real braveheart, Sir William Wallace.

Racy, blood on every page, violently anglophobic, grossly embellished, vulgar and disgusting, clumsy and stilted, a literary failure, a great epic. Whatever the verdict on BLIND HARRY, this is the book which has done more than any other to frame the notion of Scotland's national identity. Despite its numerous 'historical inaccuracies', it remains the principal source for what we now know about the life of Wallace.

The novel and film *Braveheart* were based on the 1722 Hamilton edition of this epic poem. Burns, Wordsworth, Byron and others were greatly influenced by this version 'wherein the old obsolete words are rendered more intelligible', which is said to be the book, next to the Bible, most commonly found in Scottish households in the eighteenth century. Burns even admits to having 'borrowed... a couplet worthy of Homer' directly from Hamilton's version of BLIND HARRY to include in 'Scots wha hae'.

Elspeth King, in her introduction to this, the first accessible edition of BLIND HARRY in verse form since 1859, draws parallels between the situation in Scotland at the time of Wallace and that in Bosnia and Chechnya in the 1990s. Seven hundred years to the day after the Battle of Stirling Bridge, the 'Settled Will of the Scottish People' was expressed in the devolution referendum of 11 September 1997. She describes this as a landmark opportunity for mature reflection on how the nation has been shaped, and sees BLIND HARRY'S WALLACE as an essential and compelling text for this purpose.

On the Trail of William Wallace

David R. Ross

ISBN 0 946487 47 2 PBK £7.99

How close to reality was *Braveheart*?

Where was Wallace actually born?

What was the relationship between Wallace and Bruce?

Are there any surviving eye-witness accounts of Wallace?

How does Wallace influence the psyche of today's Scots?

On the Trail of William Wallace offers a refreshing insight into the life and heritage of the great Scots hero whose proud story is at the very heart of what it means to be Scottish. Not concentrating simply on the hard historical facts of Wallace's life, the book also takes into account the real significance of Wallace and his effect on the ordinary Scot through the ages, manifested in the many sites where his memory is marked.

In trying to piece together the jigsaw of the reality of Wallace's life, David Ross weaves a subtle flow of new information with his own observations. His engaging, thoughtful and at times amusing narrative reads with the ease of a historical novel, complete with all the intrigue, treachery and romance required to hold the attention of the casual reader and still entice the more knowledgable historian.

74 places to visit in Scotland and the north of England

One general map and 3 location maps

Stirling and Falkirk battle plans

Wallace's route through London

Chapter on Wallace connections in North America and elsewhere

Reproductions of rarely seen illustrations

On the Trail of William Wallace will be enjoyed by anyone with an interest in Scotland, from the passing tourist to the most fervent nationalist. It is an encyclopaedia-cum-guide book, literally stuffed with fascinating titbits not usually on offer in the conventional history book.

Luath Press Limited
committed to publishing well written books worth reading

LUATH PRESS takes its name from Robert Burns, whose little collie Luath (*Gael.*, swift or nimble) tripped up Jean Armour at a wedding and gave him the chance to speak to the woman who was to be his wife and the abiding love of his life. Burns called one of *The Twa Dogs* Luath after Cuchullin's hunting dog in *Ossian's Fingal*. Luath Press was established in 1981 in the heart of Burns country, and is now based a few steps up the road from Burns' first lodgings on Edinburgh's Royal Mile.

Luath offers you distinctive writing with a hint of unexpected pleasures.

Most bookshops in the UK, the US, Canada, Australia, New Zealand and parts of Europe either carry our books in stock or can order them for you. To order direct from us, please send a £sterling cheque, postal order, international money order or your credit card details (number, address of cardholder and expiry date) to us at the address below. Please add post and packing as follows: UK – £1.00 per delivery address; overseas surface mail – £2.50 per delivery address; overseas airmail – £3.50 for the first book to each delivery address, plus £1.00 for each additional book by airmail to the same address. If your order is a gift, we will happily enclose your card or message at no extra charge.

Luath Press Limited
543/2 Castlehill
The Royal Mile
Edinburgh EH1 2ND
Scotland
Telephone: 0131 225 4326 (24 hours)
Fax: 0131 225 4324
email: gavin.macdougall@luath.co.uk
Website: www.luath.co.uk